ETHNICITY AND AGING:
A BIBLIOGRAPHY

ETHNICITY AND AGING:
A BIBLIOGRAPHY

Compiled by
Edward Murguía
Tena M. Schultz
Kyriakos S. Markides
Philip Janson

TRINITY UNIVERSITY PRESS • SAN ANTONIO, TEXAS

Ref.
HQ
1064
.U5
E85
1984

Checklists in the Humanities and Education: a Series

Harry B. Caldwell, Trinity University, General Editor

As a continuing effort, *Checklists in the Humanities and Education: a Series* endeavors to provide the student and academician with essential bibliographical information on important scholarly subjects not readily available in composite form. The series emphasizes selection and limitation of both primary and secondary works, providing a practical research tool as a primary aim. For example, this volume deals only with American elderly ethnic and racial groups and lists titles that are readily accessible to the user, excluding unpublished papers, conference reports, in-house documents, and other such materials. Likewise, subsequent volumes will remain selective, limited, and concise.

Library of Congress Cataloging in Publication Data
Main entry under title:

Ethnicity and aging.

(Checklists in the humanities and education; 8)
Includes index.
1. Aged–United States–Bibliography. 2. Minority aged–United States–Bibliography. 3. Ethnicity–United States–Bibliography. I. Murguia, Edward. II. Series.
Z7164.04E85 1983   016.3052'6'0973   83-18273
[HQ1064.U5]
ISBN 0-939980-03-7

© Copyright 1984 Edward Murguía, Tena M. Schultz, Kyriakos S. Markides, Philip Janson
ISBN 0-939980-03-7

Manufactured in the United States of America

Printed by Best Printing Company
Bound by Custom Bookbinders

Trinity University Press, 715 Stadium Drive
San Antonio, Texas 78284

Contents

Preface

The purpose of this volume is to assist researchers, teachers, and policy-makers by presenting a comprehensive but selective, up-to-date, multiethnic bibliography on aging. The need for such a tool has arisen because of the increase in size of the minority elderly population as well as society's growing awareness of special characteristics of the group.

The intellectual importance of combining ethnic studies and gerontology reflects the growth in the last twenty years in both of these areas of academic inquiry. Beginning in the 1960s, a number of historical circumstances encouraged a reawakening of the importance of ethnic and racial differences to an understanding of social life in the United States. Prominent among these were the racial disturbances in numerous American cities in which hundreds of people were injured or killed and millions of dollars in property damage inflicted. These events led an entire society to reexamine its foundation as well as its course. Also related were the civil rights and ethnic awareness movements, in particular the Black, Chicano, and American Indian movements.

Concurrently there was a marked rise in the percentage of minority populations living in politically important central cities. It became evident that while the proportion of the old that could be classified as poor decreased throughout the post-war era, such gains have been more elusive among the minority elderly. Together, these factors—the increase in numbers and the economic implications—broadly described as they are here, at least partially account for the emphasis on studying ethnicity and aging in American society. Consequently, what has emerged are federally funded research projects, large-scale social policy initiatives, and courses of study leading to the bachelor and masters degrees in gerontology.

As researchers attempt to intersect these two fields of study, they discover both theoretical and methodological problems. Most of these are reflected in the literature and are therefore worth some description here. Current theories on aging continue to wrestle with the relative importance of ethnicity vs. social class. Since for many researchers old age implies a continuation of stratification disadvantages, the life styles and life chances of the minority old are often thought of as being primarily attributable to their social class standing (Markides, 1982).

Others, however, have long maintained that even after one "controls" for social class, important differences due to ethnicity and/or race remain (Willie, 1979). Along these lines it should be noted that no other population segment is more culturally distinct than the old. More than any other age group, older ethnics are more likely to possess attitudes and behavior associated with their ethnic and/or racial group, ways of thinking and acting present in perhaps only attenuated forms among their offspring. The study of aging and ethnicity in the same context, then, directly addresses the theoretical problem of untangling (now three legs) of what has been called a multiple stratification hierarchy (Jeffries and Ransford, 1980): age, ethnicity, and social class.

As with any bibliography, we were faced with a number of decisions regarding the inclusion or exclusion of documents. The criteria chosen was that all citations in this bibliography deal only with American elderly ethnic and racial groups and that each document be readily accessible to the user, thus excluding all unpublished papers, conference reports, in-house documents, etc.

Our method of finding relevant literature included a search of existing bibliographies, textbooks, government reports, technical documents, and scholarly journals in the social, behavioral, and medical sciences. We used a variety of electronic data bases. We wrote several of the most prominent and productive researchers in the field for citations of their most recent publications. In order to add to the long-term usefulness of this volume, we have included a listing of the sources and computer searches that yielded a substantial number of the entries. Periodic checks of these resources will enable the reader to keep this bibliography current.

In addition to our attempt to compile a current resource document, we tried to organize the material to be as serviceable as possible for the user. The bibliography is divided into ethnic and racial categories and within those into topical areas. Within each subject grouping, items are arranged alphabetically by author's name. Thus, the researcher should have little difficulty in finding relevant citations under such topics as "Hispanic: Health, Medicine, and Folk Medicine: or "Native American: Death and Dying." (Incidentally this arrangement by ethnicity and subject area also lends itself to an identification of research gaps. We identified no research, for example, on Hispanics and Food and Nutrition and found a paucity of work in general on white ethnics.) Finally, we have included an author index.

We would like to thank the following for their support and assistance. Lois Boyd, director of Trinity University Press, encouraged this project from the beginning, as did Charles B. White, director of the Gerontology Program at Trinity. Thomas C. Greaves, dean, Division of Behavioral Sciences, provided us with funds by which this manuscript could be placed on a word processor, greatly facilitating the editing. Norma J. Carmack, social science librarian at Trinity, assisted us with electronic literature searches. Elizabeth Treviño most competently transcribed a large part of the material from handwritten cards onto a word processor and made corrections on subsequent drafts. Beatrice Fagan, secretary, Department of Sociology, aided us in numerous ways, from clerical assistance to moral support. Harry B. Caldwell, general editor of Checklists in the Humanities and Education, has been a most helpful editor. We also appreciate those writers who responded to our inquiries with their current titles.

While the above should take credit for the positive aspects of this compilation, its errors and shortcomings remain ours.

References

Jeffries, V., and Ransford, H. E., *Social Stratification: A Multiple Hierarchy Approach.* Boston: Allyn & Bacon, 1980.

Markides, K. S., "Minority Aging," in M. W. Riley, B. B. Hess, and K. Bond, eds. *Aging in Society: Selected Reviews of Recent Research.* Hillsdale, N.J.: Lawrence Erlbaum Associates, 1983.

Willie, C. V., *The Caste and Class Controversy.* Bayside, New York: General Hall, 1979.

Compilers

Edward Murguía, associate professor of sociology, Trinity University, holds the Ph.D. degree from the University of Texas at Austin. He is the author of *Assimilation, Colonialism and the Mexican American People* (1975) and *Chicano Intermarriage: A Theoretical and Empirical Study* (1982). His articles have appeared in *Social Science Quarterly* and *Marriage and Family Review.*

Tena M. Schultz, currently a case worker with Ramparts, a program to provide services for the elderly, is also an M.A. candidate in the Gerontology Program at Trinity University. She holds the B.A. degree from the University of Texas at San Antonio.

Kyriakos S. Markides, associate professor, Division of Sociomedical Sciences, Department of Preventive Medicine and Community Health, University of Texas Medical Branch at Galveston, holds the Ph.D. degree from Louisiana State University. He has published extensively in the area of ethnicity and aging in such journals as *Social Science Quarterly, Journal of Gerontology, The Gerontologist, Research on Aging, International Journal of Aging and Human Development,* and many others. His essays have appeared in various collective works. His recent book with Harry W. Martin is entitled *Older Mexican Americans: A Study in an Urban Barrio.*

Philip Janson received his Ph.D. from the University of Southern California. He has published articles in a number of scholarly journals including *Social Forces, The Gerontologist* and *Research on Aging.* His current research is focused on the effect of population aging on minority residential succession. In addition, he has published articles on ethnic differences in well-being and on fear of crime among the elderly.

ETHNICITY AND AGING:
A BIBLIOGRAPHY

I. Multiethnic and General Studies

Crime, Prisons, and the Legal System

1. Gilfix, M. "Minority Elders: Legal Problems and the Need for Legal Services." In *Comprehensive Service Delivery Systems for the Minority Aged*, ed. by E. P. Stanford. San Diego: San Diego State University, 1977.

2. Hays, D., and Wisotsk, M. "The Aged Offender: A Review of the Literature and Two Current Studies from the New York State Division of Parole." *Journal of American Geriatrics Society*, *17* (1969): 1064-73.

3. Janson, P., and Ryder, L. "Crime and the Elderly: The Relationship Between Risk and Fear." *Gerontologist*, *23*, no. 2 (1983): 207-12.

4. Lawton, M. "Victimization and Fear of Crime in Elderly Public Housing Tenants." *Journal of Gerontology*, *35*, no. 5 (1980): 768-79.

5. Peek, C.; Alton, J.; and Lowe, G. "Comparative Evaluation of the Local Police." *Public Opinion Quarterly*, *42*, no. 3 (1978): 370-79.

6. Ragan, P. "Crime Against the Elderly: Findings from Interviews with Blacks, Mexican Americans and Whites." In *Justice and Older Americans*, ed. by M. A. Y. Rifai. Lexington, Mass.: D. C. Heath, 1977.

7. Rifai, M. A. Y., ed. *Justice and Older Americans*. Lexington, Mass.: D. C. Heath, 1977.

8. Yin, P. "Fear of Crime Among the Elderly: Some Issues and Suggestions." *Social Problems*, *27*, no. 4 (1980): 492-504.

Death and Dying

9. Bengtson, V.; Cuellar, J.; and Ragan, P. "Stratum Contrasts and Similarities in Attitudes toward Death by Race, Age, Social Class and Sex." *Journal of Gerontology*, *32*, no. 1 (1977): 76-88. See also: Demographic and Socioeconomic Characteristics.

10. Fitzgerald, E. "Southwestern Perspectives on the Resolution of Grief." In *Acute Grief and the Funeral*, ed. by V. Pine, A. Kutschen, D. Peretz, R. Slater, R. Bellis, R. Valk, and D. Cherico. Springfield, Ill.: Charles C. Thomas, 1976.

11. Goldberg, H. "Funeral and Bereavement Rituals of Kota Indians and Orthodox Jews." *Omega*, *12*, no. 2 (1981-82): 117-28.

12. Gutmann, D. "The Premature Gerontology: Themes of Aging and Death in the Youth Culture." In *Death in American Experience*, ed. by A. Mack. New York: Shocken Books, 1973.

13.   Harper, B. C. "Some Snapshots of Death and Dying Among Ethnic Minorities." In *Minority Aging: Sociological and Social Psychological Issues*, ed. by R. C. Manuel. Westport: Greenwood Press, 1982.

14.   Kalish, R., and Reynolds, D. K. *Death and Ethnicity: A Psychocultural Study.* Los Angeles: The Ethel Percy Andrus Gerontology Center, University of Southern California, 1976.

15.   _____. "The Role of Age in Death Attitudes." *Death Education*, 1, no. 2 (1977): 205-30.

16.   Kastenbaum, R. "Reflections on Old Age, Ethnicity, and Death." In *Ethnicity and Aging: Theory, Research and Policy*, ed. by D. E. Gelfand and A. J. Kutzik. New York: Springer, 1979.

17.   Keily, M., and Dudek, S. "Attitudes toward Death in Aged Persons." *Psychiatric Journal of the University of Ottowa*, 2, no. 4 (1977): 181-84.

18.   Kubler-Ross, E., ed. *Death: The Final Stage of Growth.* Englewood Cliffs: Prentice-Hall, 1975.

19.   Lanceford, R., and Lanceford, J. *Attitudes on Death and Dying: A Cross Cultural View.* Los Angeles: Hwong, 1976.

20.   Lister, L. "Cultural Perspectives on Death as Viewed from Within a Skilled Nursing Facility." In *Social Work with the Dying Patient and the Family.* New York: Columbia University Press, 1977.

21.   Lopata, H. *Widowhood in an American City.* Cambridge: Schenkman, 1972.

22.   McIntosh, J., and Santos, J. "Suicide Among Minority Elderly—A Preliminary Investigation." *Suicide and Life-Threatening Behavior, 11* (1981): 151-66.

23.   Mack, A., ed. *Death in American Experience.* New York: Shocken Books, 1973.

24.   Myers, J.; Wass, H.; and Murphey, M. "Ethnic-Differences in Death Anxiety Among Elderly." *Death Education, 4*, no. 3 (1980): 237-44.

25.   Pine, V.; Kutschen, A.; Peretz, D.; Slater, R.; Bellis, R.; Valk, R.; and Cherico, D., eds. *Acute Grief and the Funeral.* Springfield, Illinois: Charles C. Thomas, 1976.

26.   Saunders, J.; Poole, T.; and Rivero, W. T. "Death Anxiety Among the Elderly." *Psychological Reports, 46*, no. 1 (1980): 53-54.

27.   Seiden, R. H. "Mellowing with Age: Factors Influencing the Nonwhite Suicide Rate." *International Journal of Aging and Human Development, 13*, no. 4 (1981): 265-84.

28.   Watson, W., and Maxwell, R. *Human Aging and Dying: A Study in Sociocultural Gerontology.* New York: St. Martin's Press, 1977.

Demographic and Socioeconomic Characteristics

29.   Barron, M. "Minority Group Characteristics of the Aged in American Society." *Journal of Gerontology,* 8, no. 4 (1953): 477-82.

30.   Blau, Z.; Oser, G.; and Stephens, R. "Aging, Social Class, and Ethnicity: A Comparison of Anglo, Black, and Mexican-American Texans." *Pacific Sociological Review,* 22, no. 4 (1979): 501-25.

31.   Carp, F. "The Mobility of Older Slum-Dwellers." *Gerontologist,* 12 (1972): 57-65.

32.   Fowles, D. "Income and Poverty Among the Elderly: 1975." Washington, D.C.: U.S. Government Printing Office, 1977.

33.   Fujii, S. "Minority Group Elderly: Demographic Characteristics and Implications for Public Policy." In *Annual Review of Gerontology and Geriatrics.* Vol. 1. Ed. by C. Eisdorfer. New York: Springer, 1980. See also: Social Policy and Politics.

34.   Giles, H. F. "Differential Life Expectancy Among White and Non-white Americans: Some Explanations During Youth and Middle Age." In *Minority Aging: Sociological and Social Psychological Issues,* ed. by R. C. Manuel. Westport: Greenwood Press, 1982.

35.   Heyman, D., and Jeffers, F. "Study of the Relative Influence of Race and Socioeconomic Status upon the Activities and Attitudes of a Southern Aged Population." *Journal of Gerontology,* 19 (1964): 225-29. See also: Social Participation and Friendships.

36.   Lee, A. "Return Migration in the United States." *International Migration Review,* 8, no. 2 (1974): 283-300.

37.   Manton, K. G. "Differential Life Expectancy: Possible Explanations During the Late Ages." In *Minority Aging: Sociological and Social Psychological Issues,* ed. by R. C. Manuel. Westport: Greenwood Press, 1982.

38.   Manuel, R. C., and Reid, J. "A Comparative Demographic Profile of the Minority and Nonminority Aged." In *Minority Aging: Sociological and Social Psychological Issues,* ed. by R. C. Manuel. Westport: Greenwood Press, 1982.

39.   Munick, W., and Sullivan, D. "Race, Age, and Family Status Differentials in Metropolitan Migration of Households." *Rural Sociology,* 42, no. 4 (1977): 536-43.

40. Siegel, J. "Estimates of Coverage of the Population by Sex, Race, and Age in the 1970 Census." *Demography, 11* (1974): 1-23.

41. Thomas, G. "Regional Migration Patterns and Poverty Among the Aged in the South." *Journal of Human Resources, 8* (1973): 73-84.

42. U.S. Bureau of the Census. *Demographic Aspects of Aging and the Older Population in the United States.* Current Population Reports, Series P-23, no. 59. Washington, D.C.: U.S. Government Printing Office, 1971.

43. _____. *"Estimates of the Population of the U.S. by Age, Sex, and Race: 1970-1977."* Current Population Reports, Series P-25, no. 721. Washington, D.C.: U.S. Government Printing Office, 1978.

44. Warheit, G.; Holzer, C.; and Schwab, J. "An Analysis of Social Class and Racial Differences in Depressive Symptomatology: A Community Study." *Journal of Health and Social Behavior, 14,* no. 4 (1973): 291-99. See also: Mental Health and Life Satisfaction.

Education

45. Fritz, D. "Educational Preparation of Practitioners to Work with the Minority Elderly: Considerations for Program Development." In *Research and Training in Minority Aging,* ed. by G. A. Sherman. Washington, D.C.: The National Center on the Black Aged, 1978.

46. Hartford, M. "Curriculum Development for the Preparation of Practitioners to Work with Minority Elderly." In *Research and Training in Minority Aging,* ed. by G. A. Sherman. Washington, D.C.: National Center on the Black Aged, 1978.

47. Heisel, M. A. "Adult Education and the Disadvantaged Older Adult: An Analytical Review of the Research Literature." *Educational Gerontology, 5,* no. 2 (1980): 125-37.

48. Ishikawa, W. "Curriculum Development." In *Minority Aging: Institute on Minority Aging Proceedings,* ed. by E. P. Stanford. San Diego: San Diego State University, 1974.

49. Jackson, J. "Education and Training Priorities for Ethnic Groups." In *Conferences on the Role of Institutions of Higher Learning in the Study of Aging, 1972,* ed. by R. H. Davis, et al. Los Angeles: The Ethel Percy Andrus Gerontology Center, University of Southern California, 1973.

50. Lipman, A. "Ethnic and Minority Group Content for Courses in Aging." In *Gerontology in Higher Education: Perspectives and Issues,*

Papers from the 1977 Meeting of the Association for Gerontology in Higher Education, ed. by M. M. Seltzer, et al. Belmont, Calif.: Wadsworth, 1978.

51.　Pratt, C. "Minority Aging: Education in a Majority Institution." *Gerontology and Geriatric Education,* 2, no. 3 (1982): 171-77.

52.　Pritchard, D. "Minority Older Persons in Adult Educational Programs." In *Retirement: Concepts and Realities,* ed. by E. P. Stanford. San Diego: San Diego State University, 1978.

53.　Schmall, V., and Staton, M. "A Minority Cultural Experience for University Gerontology Students." *Educational Gerontology,* 6, no. 4 (1981): 365-71.

54.　Schwartz, B., ed. "Utilization of College Resources." In *Gerontology: A Program Guide.* Upper Montclair: Montclair State College, 1976.

55.　Smith, S. "The Developing Gerontological Training Program at Fisk University." In *Proceedings of the Research Conference on Minority Group Aged in the South,* ed. by J. J. Jackson. Durham: Duke University Medical Center, 1972.

56.　Stanford, E. P. "Involving the Community in Developing Educational Programs in Minority Aging." In *Research and Training in Minority Aging,* ed. by G. A. Sherman. Washington, D.C: The National Center on the Black Aged, 1978.

57.　Sterns, H.; Ansello, E.; Sprouse, B.; and Layfield-Faux, R. M., eds. *Gerontology in Higher Education.* Belmont, Calif.: Wadsworth, 1979.

58.　Sweeney, S. M. "New Directions for the Administration on Aging Education and Training Program." *Educational Gerontology,* 5, no. 1 (1980): 1-15. See also: Theory, Research, and Training.

59.　Tallmer, M. "Some Factors in the Education of Older Members of Minority Groups." *Journal of Geriatric Psychiatry,* 10, no. 1 (1977): 89-98.

Food and Nutrition

60.　Frederick, H. "Solving the Food Crisis for Minority Senior Citizens." In *Comprehensive Service Delivery Systems for the Minority Aged,* ed. by E. P. Stanford. San Diego: San Diego State University, 1977.

61.　Hamill, I.; Schutz, H. G.; Standa, B. R.; Day, M. L.; and Yearick, E. S. "Nutritional-Status Studies in the Western Region: Selected Ethnic and Elderly Groups." *Nutrition Reports International,* 25, no. 1 (1982): 189-99.

62. Lang, C. "Some Nutritional Aspects of the Elderly." In *Minority Aging: Policy Issues for the '80's*, ed. by E. P. Stanford. San Diego: San Diego State University, 1980.

63. West, K., et al. "Nutritional Factors in the Etiology of Diabetes." In *Epidemiology of Diabetes*, ed. by H. Keen. Geneva: World Health Organization, 1978. See also: Health, Medicine, and Folk Medicine.

64. Winick, M., ed. *Nutrition and Aging*. New York: John Wiley and Sons, 1976.

General

65. Administration on Aging. *Indicators of the Status of the Elderly in the United States*. Department of HEW, Administration on Aging, 1971.

66. Atchley, R., and Seltzer, M. *Sociology of Aging: Selected Readings*. Belmont, Calif.: Wadsworth, 1976.

67. Baroni, G., and Green, G. "Who's Left in the Neighborhoods." Washington, D.C.: National Center for Urban Ethnic Affairs, 1976.

68. Barret, J. *Gerontological Psychology*. Springfield, Ill.: Charles C. Thomas, 1972.

69. Barrow, G., and Smith, P. *Aging, Ageism and Society*. St. Paul: West Publishing Co., 1979.

70. Bates, J. "Local Directions in Aging." In *Minority Aging Research: Old Issues—New Approaches*, ed. by E. P. Stanford. San Diego: San Diego State University, 1979.

71. Bell, B. "The Minority Elderly." In *Contemporary Social Gerontology*, ed. by B. Bell. Springfield, Ill.: Charles C. Thomas, 1976.

72. Bengtson, V. "Ethnicity and Perceptions of Aging." In *Aging: Challenges to Science and Social Policy*, ed. by M. Mariot. Assen, Netherlands: Royal Van Gorkum Press, 1978.

73. Blau, Z. *Aging in a Changing Society*. 2d ed. New York: Franklin Watts, 1981.

74. Bourg, C. "Elderly in a Southern Metropolitan Area." *Gerontologist*, *15* (1975): 15-22.

75. Boyer, L., and Boyer, R. "Understanding the Individual Through Folklore." *Contemporary Psychoanalysis*, *13*, no. 1 (1977): 30-51.

76. Brotman, H. "Every Ninth American." In *Developments in Aging, 1979*. Washington, D.C.: U.S. Government Printing Office, 1979.

77. Burgess, E. *Aging in Western Societies*. Chicago: University of Chicago Press, 1960.

78. Busse, E., and Pfeiffer, E., eds. *Behavior and Adaptation in Late Life*. Boston: Little, Brown, 1969.

79. Butler, R. "Old Age in Your Nation's Capitol." *Aging and Human Development, 2* (1971): 197-201.

80. _____. *Why Survive? Being Old in America*. New York: Harper and Row, 1975.

81. California Legislature, Joint Committee on Aging. *Problems Confronting Elderly Ethnic Groups in California*. Sacramento: State Printer, 1973.

82. Campos, A. "Minority Aging Populations: The Urban Concentrations." In *Minority Aging Research: Old Issues—New Approaches*, ed. by E. P. Stanford. San Diego: San Diego State University, 1979.

83. Cantor, M. "Effect of Ethnicity on Lifestyles of Inner-City Elderly." *Community Planning for an Aging Society: Designing Services and Facilities*, ed. by M. Lawton, R. Newcomer, and T. Byerts. Stroudsburg, Penn.: Dowden, Hutchinson and Ross, 1976.

84. Cohen, E. *Minority Aged in America*. Ann Arbor: Institute of Gerontology, University of Michigan, 1972.

85. Cuellar, J. B.; Stanford, E. P.; and Miller-Soule, D. I., eds. *Understanding Minority Aging: Perspectives and Sources*. San Diego: San Diego State University, 1982.

86. Federal Council on the Aging. *Annual Report to the President, 1976*. Washington, D.C.: U.S. Government Printing Office, 1977.

87. Fry, C., ed. *Aging in Culture and Society: Comparative Viewpoint and Strategies*. New York: J. F. Bergin, 1980.

88. Gelfand, D. *Aging: The Ethnic Factor*. Boston: Little, Brown, 1982.

89. _____. "Ethnicity and Aging." In *Annual Review of Gerontology and Geriatrics*. Vol. 2. Ed. by C. Eisdorfer. New York: Springer, 1981.

90. Giordano, J. "Ethnics and Minorities: A Review of the Literature." *Clinical Social Work Journal, 2*, no. 3 (1974): 207-20.

91. Grissom, D. "An Overview of Aging." In *Proceedings of the Workshop Series on the Black Aged and Aging*, ed. by J. Dorsett-Robinson. Carbondale: Southern Illinois University, 1974.

92. Harris, D., and Cole, W. *Sociology of Aging.* Boston: Houghton Mifflin Co., 1980.

93. Hendricks, J., and Hendricks, C. *Aging in a Mass Society: Myths and Realities.* 2d ed. Cambridge, Mass.: Winthrop, 1982.

94. Hess, B., ed. *Growing Old in America.* New Brunswick: Transaction Books, 1976.

95. Jackson, J. *Minorities and Aging.* Belmont, Calif.: Wadsworth, 1980.

96. Kent, D. "The Elderly in Minority Groups: Variant Patterns of Aging." *Gerontologist, 11* (1971): 26-29.

97. Kitano, H., and Sue, S. "The Model Minorities." *Journal of Social Issues, 29,* no. 2 (1973): 1-9.

98. Kluckhohn, C., ed. *Culture and Behavior.* New York: The Free Press, 1962.

99. McNeely, R. and Colen, J. *Aging in Minority Groups.* Beverly Hills: Sage, 1983.

100. Markides, K. "Ethnicity and Aging: A Comment." *Gerontologist, 22* (1982): 467-70. See also: Theory, Research, and Training.

101. _____. "Minority Aging." In *Aging in Society: Reviews of Recent Literature,* ed. by M. W. Riley, B. B. Hess, and K. Bond. Hillsdale, N.J.: Lawrence Erlbaum Associates, 1983.

102. Mering, O., and Weniger, F. "Social-Cultural Background of the Aging Individual." In *Handbook of Aging and the Individual,* ed. by J. Birren. Chicago: University of Chicago Press, 1959.

103. Moriwaki, S. "Ethnicity and Aging." In *Nursing and the Aged,* ed. by I. M. Burnside. New York: McGraw-Hill, 1976.

104. Myerhoff, B., and Simic, A., eds. *Life's Career – Aging: Subcultural Variations in Growing Old.* Beverly Hills: Sage Publications, 1978.

105. National Council on the Aging. "Plight of Elderly Among Minorities." *National Council on the Aging Journal,* 1967.

106. Neugarten, B. *Middle Age and Aging: A Reader in Social Psychology.* Chicago: University of Chicago Press, 1968.

107. Newquist, D. "Aging Across Cultures." *Generations* (Summer 1977): 12-13.

108. Orbach, H., and Tibbitts, C. *Aging and the Economy.* Ann Arbor: University of Michigan Press, 1963.

109. Rabushka, A., and Jacobs, B. *Old Folks at Home.* New York: The Free Press, 1980.

110. Ragan, P., ed. *Aging Parents.* Los Angeles: University of Southern California, 1979.

111. Riley, M. W. et al. A. *Aging and Society.* 3 vols. New York: Russell Sage, 1968, 1969, 1972.

112. Riley, M. W.; Hess, B. B.; and Bond, K., eds. *Aging in Society: Selected Reviews of Recent Research.* Hillsdale, N. J.: Lawrence Erlbaum Associates, 1983.

113. Rose, A., and Peterson, W. A., eds. *Older People and Their Social World: The Subculture of the Aging.* Philadelphia: F. A. Davis, 1965.

114. Rosow, I. *Socialization to Old Age.* Berkeley: University of California Press, 1974.

115. Saltz, C.; Phillips, H.; Herndon, S.; and Gaylord, S. *Gerontopics: An Aging Resource Book.* Chapel Hill: North Carolina University, Department of Health Administration, 1980.

116. Saul, S. *Aging: An Album of People Growing Old.* New York: John Wiley, 1974.

117. Solomon, B. "Growing Old in the Ethnic-System." In *Minority Aging: Institute on Minority Aging Proceedings,* ed. by E. P. Stanford. San Diego: San Diego State University, 1974.

118. Souflee, F. "Biculturism: An Existential Phenomenon." In *Black/ Chicano Elderly: Service Delivery Within a Cultural Context,* ed. by R. Wright. Arlington: Graduate School of Social Work, The University of Texas at Arlington, 1980.

119. Speiser, A. "Another Culture, Another Time." *Journal of the American Geriatrics Society,* 22, no. 12 (1974): 551-52.

120. Stanford, E. P., ed. *Minority Aging: Institute on Minority Aging Proceedings.* San Diego: San Diego State University, 1974.

121. _____. *Minority Aging: Institute on Minority Aging Proceedings.* San Diego: San Diego State University, 1975.

122. _____. *Comprehensive Service Delivery Systems for the Minority Aged.* San Diego: San Diego State University, 1977.

123. _____. *Minority Aging: Policy Issues for the '80's.* San Diego: San Diego State University, 1980.

124. _____. *Minority Aging Research: Old Issues—New Approaches*, San Diego: San Diego State University, 1979.

125. Stephens, J. "The Aged Minority." In *Minority Aged in America: Occasional Papers in Gerontology*, no. 10. Ann Arbor: Institute of Gerontology, University of Michigan, 1971.

126. Tibbitts, C. *Handbook of Social Gerontology*. Chicago: University of Chicago Press, 1960.

127. Tibbitts, C., and Donahue, W. *Aging in Today's Society*. Englewood Cliffs: Prentice-Hall, 1960.

128. _____, eds. *Social and Psychological Aspects of Aging*. New York: Columbia University Press, 1962.

129. U.S. Senate, Special Committee on Aging. "Areas of Continuing or Emerging Concern: I. Minorities." In *Developments in Aging: 1978 (Part I)*. Washington: U.S. Government Printing Office, 1979.

130. Viscus, W., and Zeckhauser, R. *Welfare of the Elderly*. Cambridge, Mass.: Elderly Systems Inc., 1974.

131. Western Gerontological Society. "Minority Aging." Special issue of *Generations*, Quarterly Newsletter (Summer 1977).

132. Zola, I. "Oh Where, Oh Where Has Ethnicity Gone?" In *Ethnicity and Aging: Theory, Research, and Policy*, ed. by D. E. Gelfand and A. J. Kutzik. New York: Springer, 1979.

Health, Medicine, and Folk Medicine

133. Anderson, F. "Health and Environment." In *Minority Aging: Institute on Minority Aging Proceedings*, ed. by E. P. Stanford. San Diego: San Diego State University, 1974.

134. Bahr, R. T., and Gress, L. D. "Course Description: The Nursing Process: Ethnicity and Aging." *Journal of Gerontological Nursing*, 6, no. 4 (1980): 210-13.

135. Bauer, M. "Differentials in Health Characteristics by Color." U.S., July 1965-June 1967. National Center for Health Statistics, Series 10, no. 56, Oct. 1969.

136. Beaudet, F. "Physiology of Aging: Implications for Health Maintenance." In *Minority Aging: Policy Issues for the '80's*, ed. by E. P. Stanford. San Diego: San Diego State University, 1980.

137. Berk, M. L., and Bernstein, A. B. "Regular Source of Care and the Minority Aged." *Journal of the American Geriatrics Society, 30,* no. 4 (1982): 251-54.

138. Boscarino, J. "Characteristics of Patients Referred to Alcoholism Treatment Centers." *Psychological Reports, 44,* no. 3, pt. 1 (1979): 1019-20. See also: Demographic and Socioeconomic Characteristics.

139. Cantor, M., and Mayer, M. "Health and the Inner City Elderly." *Gerontologist, 16* (1976): 17-24.

140. Chapa, F. "Comprehensive Health Planning and the Minority Aged." In *Comprehensive Service Delivery Systems for the Minority Aged,* ed. by E. P. Stanford. San Diego: San Diego State University, 1977.

141. Christensen, B.; Stallones, R.; Insull, W.; Gottos, A.; and Taunton, D. "Cardiovascular Risk Factors in a Tri-Ethnic Population: Houston, Texas 1972-1975." *Journal of Chronic Diseases, 34* (1981): 105-18.

142. Darsky, B., and Weeks, H. *The Urban Aged: Race and Medical Care.* Ann Arbor: University of Michigan, School of Public Health, 1968.

143. Eve, S., and Friedsam, H. "Ethnic Differences in the Use of Health Care Services Among Older Texans." *Journal of Minority Aging, 4* (1979): 62-75.

144. Fabrega, H.; Moore, R.; and Strawn, J. "Low Income Medical Problem Patients: Some Medical and Behavioral Features." *Journal of Health and Social Behavior, 10* (1969): 334-43. See also: Demographic and Socioeconomic Characteristics.

145. French, J., and Schwartz, D. "Terminal Care at Home in Two Cultures." *American Journal of Nursing, 73* (1973): 502-5.

146. Fujii, S. "Special Case of Frailty among Minority Elderly." *Gerontologist, 17,* no. 5 (1977): 60-65.

147. German, P.; Shapiro, S.; Chase, G.; and Vollmer, M. "Health Care of the Elderly in Medically Disadvantaged Populations." *Gerontologist, 18,* no. 6 (1978): 547-55.

148. Jackson, H. "Geriatric Patients of Minority Groups." *Psychiatric Opinion, 11,* no. 2 (1974): 14-19.

149. Jackson, J. J. "Compensatory Care for Aged Minorities." In *Minority Aged in America—Occasional Papers in Gerontology, no. 10.* Ann Arbor: Institute of Gerontology, University of Michigan-Wayne State University, 1973.

150.   Lang, C. "Physiological vs. Chronological Aging and Some Implications for Health Maintenance." In *Minority Aging: Policy Issues for the '80's*, ed. by E. P. Stanford. San Diego: San Diego State University, 1980.

151.   Lawrence, P. "Health Problems of the Minority Elderly." In *Retirement: Concepts & Realities*, ed. by E. P. Stanford. San Diego: San Diego State University, 1978.

152.   Lewis, I., and Smith, L. "Health Problems of the Minority Elderly." In *Comprehensive Service Delivery Systems for the Minority Aged*, ed. by E. P. Stanford. San Diego: San Diego State Univerity, 1977.

153.   Linn, M.; Hunter, K.; and Linn, B. "Self-Assessed Health, Impairment and Disability in Anglo, Black and Cuban Elderly." *Medical Care*, 18 (1980): 282-88.

154.   Mendoza, L. "Health Care Access for Minority Elderly." *Generations*, 5, no. 2 (1980): 32.

155.   Myers, B. "The Unequal Burdens: Paying for Health Care." *Civil Rights Digest*, 10, no. 1 (1977): 12-18. See also: Prejudice, Discrimination, Racism, and Stereotyping.

156.   Nader, L., and Maritzki, T., eds. *Cultural Illness and Health*. Washington, D.C.: American Anthropological Assn., 1973.

157.   National Center for Health Statistics. *Differentials in Health Characteristics by Color, June 1965-July 1967*. Vital & Health Statistics Series 10, no. 56. Washington, D.C.: U.S. Government Printing Office, Oct. 1969.

158.   _____. *Health Characteristics of Minority Groups, United States, 1976*. Washington, D.C.: Public Health Service, Vital and Health Statistics, Advance Data, no. 27, U.S. Government Printing Office, 1978.

159.   _____. *Prevalence of Osteoarthritis in Adults by Age, Sex, Race and Geographic Area, U.S., 1960-62*. Series II, no. 15, 1966. See also: Demographic and Socioeconomic Characteristics.

160.   Newquist, D.; Berger, M.; Kahn, K.; Martinez, C.; and Burton, L. *Prescription for Neglect: Experiences of Older Blacks and Mexican-Americans with the American Health Care System*. Los Angeles: The Ethel Percy Andrus Gerontology Center, University of Southern California, 1979.

161. Nowlin, J. "Geriatric Health Status: Influence of Race and Economic Status." *Journal of Minority Aging, 4,* no. 4 (1979): 93-98. See also: Demographic and Socioeconomic Characteristics.

162. Robinson, J. "Migrant Labor and Minority Communities: Class, Ethnicity, Age, and Gender as Social Barriers to Health Care." *Journal of Health Politics, Policy and Law, 1,* no. 4 (1977): 514-22. See also: Demographic and Socioeconomic Characteristics; Prejudice, Discrimination, Racism, and Stereotyping.

163. Schafft, G. "Health Care for Racial and Ethnic Minorities and Handicapped Persons." *Journal of Long-term Care Administration, 8,* no. 4 (1980): 37-40.

164. _____. "Long-Term Care for Minorities: An Unfinished Agenda." In *Minority Aging: Policy Issues for the '80's,* ed. by E. P. Stanford. San Diego: San Diego State University, 1980.

165. Scutchfield, F. "Health Care for the Minority Aging: Institution and Home Health Services." In *Minority Aging: Policy Issues for the '80's,* ed. by E. P. Stanford. San Diego: San Diego State University, 1980.

166. Solis, F. "Health Status of Minority Elderly." In *Minority Aging Research: Old Issues—New Approaches,* ed. by E. P. Stanford. San Diego: San Diego State University, 1979.

167. Trysgstad, C. "Physiology of Aging and Health Maintenance." In *Minority Aging: Policy Issues for the '80's,* ed. by E. P. Stanford. San Diego: San Diego State University, 1980.

168. Walters, B., and Beaudet-Walters, M. "Subsidized Home Rehabilitation Programs: Minority Status—Equities and Inequities." In *Minority Aging Research: Old Issues—New Approaches,* ed. by E. P. Stanford. San Diego: San Diego State University, 1979.

169. Weeks, A., and Parsky, B. *The Urban Aged: Race and Medical Care.* Ann Arbor: University of Michigan School of Public Health, 1968.

170. Williams, D. "Considerations for Comprehensive Health Planning for Elderly Minority Populations." In *Minority Aging: Policy Issues for the '80's,* ed. by E. P. Stanford. San Diego: San Diego State University, 1980.

171. Yee, D. "Culturally Compatible Health Service." In *Minority Aging: Policy Issues for the '80's,* ed. by E. P. Stanford. San Diego: San Diego State University, 1980.

Housing

172.   Carp, F. "Housing and Minority-Group Elderly. " *Gerontologist*, 9 (1969): 20-24.

173.   Erickson, R., and Eckert, K. "The Elderly Poor in Downtown San Diego Hotels." *Gerontologist*, 17 (1977): 440-46. See also: Demographic and Socioeconomic Characteristics.

174.   Garza, J. "Ethnic Lifestyles and Housing Policy." *Generations* (Winter 1979): 32-33, 37. See also: Leisure.

175.   Golant, S. "Residential Concentrations of the Future Elderly." *Gerontologist* (Feb. Supplement 1975): 16-23.

176.   _____. "Spatial Context of Residential Moves by Elderly Persons." *Journal of Aging and Human Development*, 8, no. 3 (1977-1978): 279-89.

177.   Hoover, S. "Black and Hispanic Elderly: Their Housing Characteristics and Quality." In *Community Housing Choices for Older Americans*, ed. by M. Lawton and S. L. Hoover. New York: Springer, 1981.

178.   Martinez, C. "Policy and Research Strategies Pertinent to the Housing Needs of Minority Aged: An Example of Neglect, Inequality and Cultural Insensitivity." In *Minority Aging Research: Old Issues – New Approaches*, ed. by E. P. Stanford. San Diego: San Diego State University, 1979. See also: Prejudice, Discrimination, Racism, and Stereotyping; Social Policy and Politics.

179.   Newquist, D. "Relocation Attitudes of Older Minorities." In *Minority Aging Research: Old Issues – New Approaches*, ed. by E. P. Stanford. San Diego: San Diego State University, 1979.

180.   Soldo, B., and Lauriat, P. "Living Arrangements Among the Elderly in the United States: A Log Linear Approach." *Journal of Comparative Family Studies*, 7, no. 2 (1976): 351-66. See also: Theory, Research, and Training.

181.   Stephens, J. *Loners, Losers, and Lovers: Elderly Tenants in a Slum Hotel*. Seattle: University of Washington Press, 1980.

182.   Torres-Gil, F.; Newquist, D.; and Simonin, M. *Housing and the Diverse Aged*. Los Angeles: The Ethel Percy Andrus Gerontology Center, University of Southern California, 1978.

183.   U.S. Department of Housing and Urban Development. "Housing for the Elderly and Handicapped: The Experience of the Section 202 Program from 1959 to 1977." Washington, D.C.: Division of Policy Studies, 1979.

184.   Weeks, J. "Retirement Homes: Economic Realities and Implications for Ethnic Minority Elders." In *Retirement: Concepts and Realities*, ed. by E. P. Stanford. San Diego: San Diego State University, 1978. See also: Demographic and Socioeconomic Characteristics.

Insurance

185.   Gilfix, M. "Minority Elders: Victims of Double Discrimination in Public and Private Benefit Plans." *DePaul Law Review*, *27*, no 1 (1978): 383-405. See also: Prejudice, Discrimination, Racism, and Stereotyping.

Leisure

186.   Hutchinson, G. "Creative Use of Leisure for Aging Minorities." In *Retirement: Concepts and Realities*, ed. by E. P. Stanford. San Diego: San Diego State University, 1978. See also: Work and Retirement.

187.   Kleemeir, R., ed. *Aging and Leisure: A Research Perspective into the Meaningful Use of Time*. New York: Arno Press, 1979.

188.   Peralta, V. "Senior Centers: Reaching Minority Groups." *Aging and Leisure Living*, *3*, no. 3 (1980): 14-17.

Marriage and Family

189.   Adams, B. *Kinship in an Urban Setting*. Chicago: Markham Publishing, 1968.

190.   Allen, W. "Class, Culture, and Family Organization: The Effects of Class and Race on Family Structure in Urban America." *Journal of Comparative Family Studies*, *10* (1979): 301-13. See also: Demographic and Socioeconomic Characteristics.

191.   Duncan, G., and Morgan, J. *Five Thousand American Families – Patterns of Economic Progress*. Ann Arbor: Survey Research Center, University of Michigan, 1978.

192.   Habenstein, R., and Mindel, C. "The American Ethnic Family: Protean and Adaptive." In *Ethnic Families in America*. 2d ed. Ed. by C. Mindel and R. Habenstein. New York: Elsevier, 1981.

193.   Harris, R. "An Examination of the Effects of Ethnicity, Socioeconomic Status and Generation on Familism and Sex Role Orientations." *Journal of Comparative Family Studies*, *2* (1980): 173-93. See also: Demographic and Socioeconomic Characteristics.

194.   Mindel, C. "Extended Familism Among Urban Mexican Americans, Anglos, and Blacks." *Hispanic Journal of Behavioral Sciences, 2,* no. 1 (1980): 21-34.

195.   Mindel, C., and Habenstein, R., eds. *Ethnic Families in America,* 2d ed. New York: Elsevier, 1981.

196.   Ragan, P. "Quantitative Methods for Conducting Research on the Minority Family: Advantages and Disadvantages." In *Minority Aging Research: Old Issues—New Approaches,* ed. by E. P. Stanford. San Diego: San Diego State University, 1979. See also: Theory, Research, and Training.

197.   _____. *Aging Parents.* Los Angeles: University of California Press, 1979.

198.   Seelbach, W. "Filial Responsibility Among Aged Parents: A Racial Comparison." *Journal of Minority Aging, 5,* nos. 2-4 (1980): 266-92.

199.   Seelbach, W., and Saves, W. "Filial Responsibility Expectations and Morale Among Aged Parents." *Gerontologist, 17,* no. 6 (1977): 492-99.

200.   Spiegel, J., and Papajohn, J. *Transition in Families: A Modern Approach for Resolving Cultural and Generational Conflicts.* San Francisco: Jossey-Bass, 1975.

201.   Streib, G. F., and Beck, R. W. "Older Families: A Decade Review." *Journal of Marriage and Family, 42* (1980): 937-56.

202.   Thurber, M. "Family Patterns Vary Among U.S. Ethnic Groups." *Generations 1,* no. 2 (1982): 8-9, 38.

203.   Winch, R.; Greer, S.; and Blumberg, R. "Ethnicity and Extended Familism in an Upper-Middle Class Suburb." *American Sociological Review, 32* (1967): 265-72. See also: Demographic and Socioeconomic Characteristics.

204.   Woehrer, C. "Cultural Pluralism in American Families: The Influence of Ethnicity on Social Aspects of Aging." *Family Coordinator, 27* (1978): 329-39.

205.   _____. "The Influence of Ethnic Families on Intergenerational Relationships and Later Life Transitions." *Annals of the American Academy of Political and Social Science, 465* (November 1982): 65-78.

206.   Yelder, J. "The Natural Support System of the Family in the Lives of Ethnic Minority Elders." In *Retirement: Concepts and Realities,* ed. by E. P. Stanford. San Diego: San Diego State University, 1978.

Mental Health and Life Satisfaction

207. Blackwell, D. L., and Hunt, S. S. "Mental Health Services Reaching Out to Older Persons." *Journal of Gerontological Social Work*, 2, no. 4 (1980): 281-88.

208. Brand, F., and Smith, R. "Life Adjustment and Relocation of the Elderly." *Journal of Gerontology*, 29 (1974): 336-40. See also: Housing.

209. Butler, R., and Lewis, M. *Aging and Mental Health.* 3d ed. St. Louis: C. V. Mosby, 1982.

210. Carter, C. *Community Mental Health Programs and the Elderly. Nursing Clinics of North America, 11,* no. 1 (1976): 125-33.

211. Carter, J. H. "The Significance of Racism in the Mental Illnesses of Elderly Minorities." In *Minority Aging: Sociological and Social Psychological Issues*, ed. by R. C. Manuel. Westport, Conn.: Greenwood Press, 1982.

212. Chatfield, W. "Economic and Sociological Factors Influencing Life Satisfaction of the Aged." *Journal of Gerontology*, 32 (1977): 593-99. See also: Demographic and Socioeconomic Characteristics.

213. Chen, P. "Continuing Satisfying Life Patterns Among Aging Minorities." *Journal of Gerontological Social Work*, 2 (1980): 199-211.

214. Chevan, A., and Korson, J. "The Widowed Who Live Alone: an Examination of Social and Demographic Factors." *Social Forces*, 51 (1972): 45-53. See also: Demographic and Socioeconomic Characteristics.

215. Cool, L. E. "Ethnic Identity: A Source of Community Esteem for the Elderly." *Anthropological Quarterly*, 54, no. 4 (1981): 179-89.

216. Gaitz, C., and Scott, J. "Age and the Measurement of Mental Health." *Journal of Health and Social Behavior*, 13 (1972): 55-67.

217. Gelfand, D. "Ethnicity, Aging, and Mental Health." *International Journal of Aging and Human Development, 10,* no. 3 (1980): 289-98.

218. Gutmann, D. "Observations on Culture and Mental Health in Later Life." In *Handbook of Mental Health and Aging*, ed. by J. E. Birren and R. B. Sloane. New Jersey: Prentice-Hall, Inc., 1980.

219. Janson, P., and Frisbie, K. "Age Differences in Well-Being Among Anglos, Blacks and Mexican Americans." *Research on Aging*, 5, no. 3 (1983): 353-67.

220. Jones, E., and Korchin, S., eds. *Minority Mental Health.* New York: Holt, Rinehart and Winston, 1980.

221. Kalish, R. "A Gerontological Look at Ethnicity, Human Capacities, and Individual Adjustment." *Gerontologist, 11* (1971): 78-87.

222. Khan, N. "Mental Health Services to the Aged of Minority Groups." *Psychiatric Opinion, 11,* no. 2 (1974): 20-23.

223. Kobata, F.; Lockery, S.; and Moriwaki, S. "Minority Issues in Mental Health and Aging." In *Handbook of Mental Health and Aging,* ed. by J. E. Birren and R. B. Sloane. Englewood Cliffs: Prentice-Hall, 1980.

224. Lebowitz, B. "National Institute of Mental Health." In *Minority Aging Research: Old Issues—New Approaches,* ed. by E. P. Stanford. San Diego: San Diego State University, 1979.

225. Lenzer, A. "Social-Cultural Influences on Adjustment to Aging." *Geriatrics, 16* (1961): 631-40.

226. Levav, I., and Minami, H. "Mothers and Daughters and the Psychogeriatric Patient." *Gerontologist, 14,* no. 3 (1974): 197-200.

227. Linn, M.; Hunter, K.; and Harris, R. "Symptoms of Depression and Recent Life Events in the Community Elderly." *Journal of Clinical Psychology, 36,* no. 3 (July 1980): 675-82.

228. Linn, M.; Hunter, K; and Perry, P. "Differences by Sex and Ethnicity in the Psychosocial Adjustment of the Elderly." *Journal of Health and Social Behavior, 20,* no. 3 (1979): 273-81.

229. Linn, M.; Linn, B.; and Harris, R. "Stressful Life Events, Psychological Symptoms, and Psychosocial Adjustment in Anglo, Black, and Cuban Elderly." *Social Science and Medicine, 15E* (1981): 283-87.

230. Lowenthal, M. *Lives in Distress: The Paths of the Elderly to the Psychiatric Ward.* New York: Basic Books, 1964.

231. Lowenthal, M., and Berkman, P. *Aging and Mental Disorders in San Francisco.* San Francisco: Jossey-Bass, 1967.

232. Manuel, R. C., ed. *Minority Aging: Sociological and Social Psychological Issues.* Westport, Conn.: Greenwood Press, 1982.

233. Morgan, L. "A Re-examination of Widowhood and Morale." *Journal of Gerontology, 31* (1976): 687-95.

234. Nichols, M., and Cummins, J. "Social Adjustment of Spanish-American War Veterans." *Geriatrics, 16* (1961): 641-46.

235. Ortega, S. T.; Crutchfield, R. D; and Rushing, W. A. "Race Differences in Elderly Personal Well-Being: Friendship, Family, and Church." *Research on Aging, 5,* no. 1 (1983): 101-18. See also: Marriage and Family; Social Participation and Friendships; Religion.

236. Reynolds, D., and Kalish, R. "Anticipation of Futurity as a Function of Ethnicity and Age." *Journal of Gerontology, 29* (1974): 224-31.

237. Rosenberg, G. "Age, Poverty, and Isolation from Friends in the Urban Working Class." *Journal of Gerontology, 23,* no. 4 (1968): 533-38. See also: Demographic and Socioeconomic Characteristics.

238. Scott, J. and Gaitz, C. "Ethnic and Age Differences in Mental Health Measurements." *Diseases of the Nervous System, 36,* no. 7 (1975): 389-93.

239. Varghese, R., and Medinger, F. "Fatalism in Response to Stress Among the Minority Aged." In *Ethnicity and Aging,* ed. by D. E. Gelfand and A. J. Kutzik. New York: Springer Publishing Co., 1979.

240. Vontress, C. "Counseling Middle-Aged and Aging Cultural Minorities." *Personnel and Guidance Journal, 55,* no. 3 (1976): 132-35.

241. Watson, W. H. "Mental Health of the Minority Aged: Selected Correlates." In *Minority Aging: Sociological and Social Psychological Issues,* ed. by R. C. Manuel. Westport, Conn.: Greenwood Press, 1982.

242. Westermeyer, J., ed. *Anthropology and Mental Health.* The Hague: Mouton, 1976.

Mortality

243. Cordle, F., and Tyroler, H. "The Use of Hospital Medical Records for Epidemiologic Research. I. Differences in Hospital Utilization and In-Hospital Mortality by Age-Race-Sex-Place of Residence and Socioeconomic Status in a Defined Community Population." *Medical Care, 12,* no. 7 (1974): 596-610. See also: Demographic and Socioeconomic Characteristics; Theory, Research, and Training.

244. "Demographic and Economic Differences in Survivor Experiences in Nonwhite and White Families." *Social Security Bulletin, 43,* no. 2 (1980): 18-20. See also: Demographic and Socioeconomic Characteristics.

245. Hanlon, J. "Minority Aging Populations: Mortality and Morbidity Issues." In *Minority Aging Research: Old Issues—New Approaches,* ed. by E. P. Stanford. San Diego: San Diego State University, 1979. See also: Health, Medicine, and Folk Medicine.

246. Hechter, H., and Borhani, N. "Longevity in Racial Groups Differs." *California Health, 20,* no. 15 (1965).

247. Lee, E.; Roberts, R.; and Labrathe, D. "Excess and Deficit Lung Cancer Mortality in Three Ethnic Groups in Texas." *Cancer, 38* (1976): 2551-56. See also: Health, Medicine, and Folk Medicine.

248.   Markides, K. "Mortality Patterns and Trends Among Minority Populations." *Public Health Reports,* 98, no. 3 (1983): 252-60.

249.   Metropolitan Life Insurance Co. "Mortality Differentials Among Non-White Groups. *Statistical Bulletin,* 55 (1974): 5-8.

250.   _____. "Regional Variations in Non-White Mortality." *Statistical Bulletin,* 54 (1973): 7-9.

251.   _____. "Survival After Midlife Among Non-Whites." *Metropolitan Life Insurance Co. Statistical Bulletin* 58 (1977): 10-11.

252.   Roberts, R., and Askew, C. "A Consideration of Mortality in Three Subcultures." *Health Services Reports,* 87, no. 3 (1972): 262-70.

253.   Roberts, R.; McBee, G.; and MacDonald, E. "Social Status, Ethnic Status, and Urban Mortality: An Ecological Analysis." *Texas Reports on Biology and Medicine,* 28 (1970): 13-29. See also: Demographic and Socioeconomic Characteristics.

Nursing Homes and Institutionalization

254.   "An Administrator's Viewpoint of Long Term Care for the Minority Elderly: An Interview with Houston Baker." *Journal of Long-Term Care Administration,* 8, no. 4 (1980): 33-36.

255.   Chee, P., and Kane, R. "Cultural Factors Affecting Nursing-Home Care for Minorities: A Study of Black American and Japanese American Groups." *Journal of the American Geriatrics Society, 31,* no. 2 (1983): 109-12.

256.   Crumbaugh, M. S., ed. *Mental Health: Principles and Training Techniques in Nursing Home Care.* Rockville, Md.: National Institute of Mental Health, 1972. See also: Mental Health and Life Satisfaction.

257.   Dominick, J. "Mental Patients in Nursing Homes: Four Ethnic Influences." *Journal of American Geriatric Society, 17* (1969). See also: Mental Health and Life Satisfaction.

258.   Henry, J. *Culture Against Man.* New York: Random House, 1963.

259.   Ingram, D. K. "Profile of Chronic Illness in Nursing Homes, United States, August 1973-April, 1974." *Vital and Health Statistics,* Series 13, no. 29, Department of Health, Education and Welfare Publication (PHS) 78-1780. Hyattville, Md.: National Center for Health Statistics, 1977. See also: Health, Medicine, and Folk Medicine.

260.   Kosberg, J. I. "Differences in Proprietary Institutions Caring For Affluent and Non-affluent Elderly." Part 1. *Gerontology, 13,* no. 3 (1973): 299-304.

261.   Markson, E. W. "Ethnicity as a Factor in the Institutionalization of the Ethnic Elderly." In *Ethnicity and Aging*, ed. by D. E. Gelfand and A. J. Kutzik. New York: Springer Publishing Co., 1979.

262.   "Minorities and How They Grow Old." *Nursing Home*, 29, no. 6 (1980): 5.

263.   Morrison, B. J. "Sociocultural Dimensions: Nursing-Homes and the Minority Aged." *Journal of Gerontological Social Work*, 5, nos. 1-2 (1982): 127-45.

264.   Moss, F., and Halamandaris, V. J. *Too Old, Too Sick, Too Bad: Nursing Homes in America*. Germantown, Md.: Aspen Systems Corp., 1977.

265.   Pfeiffer, Eric, ed. *National Conference on Alternatives to Institutional Care for Older Americans: Practice and Planning*. Durham: Duke University, 1973. See also: Social Policy and Politics.

266.   Rinck, C. M.; Willis, F. N.; and Dean, L. M. "Interpersonal Touch Among Residents of Homes for the Elderly." *Journal of Communication*, 30, no. 2 (1980): 44-47.

267.   Schafft, G. "Nursing Home Care and the Minority Elderly." *Journal of Long-Term Care Administration*, 8, no. 4 (1980): 1-31.

268.   Tobin, S. *Last Home for the Aged: Critical Implications of Institutionalization*. San Francisco: Jossey-Bass,1976.

269.   U.S. Senate, Special Committee on Aging. *Access of Minority Groups to Nursing Homes*. Hearings before the Subcommittee on Long-term Care, 1972.

270.   U.S. Senate Subcommittee on Long-Term Care. "Abstract of Supporting Paper No. 8: Access to Nursing Homes by U.S. Minorities." In *Nursing Home Care in the United States: Failure in Public Policy Supporting Paper*. Washington D.C.: U.S. Government Printing Office, 1975.

Prejudice, Discrimination, Racism, and Stereotyping

271.   Allen, J., and Burwell, N. "Ageism and Racism: Two Issues in Social Work Education and Practice." *Journal of Education for Social Work*, 16 (1980): 71-77. See also: Support Services and Service Delivery.

272.   Carter, J. H. "Psychiatry, Racism, and Aging." *Journal of American Geriatrics Society*, 20 (1972): 343-46. See also: Mental Health and Life Satisfaction.

273.   Dowd, J. J. "Prejudice and Proximity." *Research on Aging*, 2 (1980): 23-48.

274. Dowd, J. J., and Bengtson, V. L. "Aging in Minority Populations: Examination of the Double Jeopardy Hypothesis." *Journal of Gerontology, 33,* no. 3 (1978): 427-36.

275. Hopkins, T. J. "A Conceptual Framework for Understanding the Three 'Isms'—Racism, Ageism, Sexism." *Journal of Education for Social Work, 16,* no. 2 (1980): 63-70. See also: Theory, Research, and Training.

276. Jackson, H. C. "Overcoming Racial Barriers in Senior Centers." *National Conference on Senior Centers, 2* (1965): 20-28.

277. Kasschau, P. "Age and Race Discrimination Reported by Middle Aged and Older Persons." *Social Forces, 55* (1977): 728-42.

278. Markides, K. S. "Health, Income and the Minority Aged: A Reexamination of the Double Jeopardy Hypothesis." *Journal of Gerontology, 36* (1981): 494-95. See also: Health, Medicine, and Folk Medicine; Demographic and Socioeconomic Characteristics.

279. Mindiola, T. "Age and Income Discrimination Against Mexican Americans and Blacks in Texas, 1960 and 1970." *Social Problems, 27,* no. 2 (1979): 196-208.

280. Morgan, W. E. "Equal Opportunity for Minority Elderly: An Inquiry." In *Minority Aging Research: Old Issues—New Approaches,* ed. by E. P. Stanford. San Diego: San Diego State University, 1979.

281. National Council on the Aging. *Triple Jeopardy: Myth or Reality?* Washington, D.C.: National Council on Aging, 1972.

282. Perry, J. S., and Cowburn, J. C. "Immigrant and Native-born American Attitudes Toward Aged." *Psychological Reports, 46,* no. 2 (1980): 549-50.

283. Ramos, R. "Being Old and Being a Minority: The Double Whammy." In *Black/Chicano Elderly: Service Delivery Within a Cultural Context,* ed. by R. Wright, Jr. Arlington, Texas: Graduate School of Social Work, The University of Texas at Arlington, 1980.

284. Saenz, D. "Triple Jeopardy: Myth or Reality." In *Triple Jeopardy: Myth or Reality?* Washington, D.C.: National Council on the Aging, 1972.

285. Schwitters, S. "Young Thoughts on the Old." *Aging* (July-August 1980): 8-13.

286. Youmans, E. G. "Age Group, Values and the Future." In *Triple Jeopardy; Myth or Reality?* Washington, D.C.: National Council on the Aging, 1972.

Religion

287. Kenney, B. P.; Vaughan, C. E.; and Cromwell, R. E. "Identifying the Socio-Contextual Forms of Religiosity Among the Urban Ethnic Minority Group Members." *Journal for the Scientific Study of Religion,* 16, no. 3 (1977): 237-44.

288. Kobata, F. S. "The Role of the Church as a Natural Support System." In *Retirement: Concepts and Realities,* ed. by E. P. Stanford. San Diego: San Diego State University, 1978. See also: Support Services and Service Delivery.

Rural

289. Donnenwerth, C.; Guy, R.; and Norwell, M. "Life Satisfaction Among Older Persons: Rural-Urban and Racial Comparisons." *Social Science Quarterly,* 59 (1978): 578-83. See also: Mental Health and Life Satisfaction.

290. Guidotti, T. L. "Health Care for a Rural Minority." *California Medicine,* 118 (1973): 98-104. See also: Health, Medicine, and Folk Medicine.

291. Kivett, V. R. "Discriminators of Loneliness Among the Rural Elderly: Implications for Intervention." *Gerontologist,* 19, no. 1 (1979): 108-15. See also: Mental Health and Life Satisfaction.

292. Kivett, V. R., and Scott, J. P. *The Rural By-passed Elderly: Perspectives on Status and Needs.* Greensboro: North Carolina Agricultural Research Service, University of North Carolina at Greensboro, 1979.

293. Menks, F.; Sittler, S.; Weaver, D.; and Yanow, B. "A Psychogeriatric Activity Group in a Rural Community." *American Journal of Occupational Therapy,* 31, no. 6 (1977): 381-84. See also: Mental Health and Life Satisfaction.

294. Youmans, E. G., ed. *Older Rural Americans.* Lexington: University of Kentucky Press, 1967.

Social Participation and Friendships

295. Cantor, M. H. "Life Space and the Social Support System of the Inner City Elderly of New York." *Gerontologist,* 15, no. 1 (1975): 23-27.

296. _____. "The Informal Support System of New York's Inner City Elderly: Is Ethnicity a Factor?" In *Ethnicity and Aging,* ed. by D. E. Gelfand and A. J. Kutzik. New York: Springer, 1979.

297.   Guttmann, D. *Informal and Formal Support Systems and Their Effect on the Lives of the Elderly in Selected Ethnic Groups.* Washington, D.C.: Catholic University of America, 1979. See also: Support Services and Service Delivery.

298.   Hoyt, D. R., and Babchuk, N. "Ethnicity and the Voluntary Associations of the Aged." *Ethnicity*, 8, no. 1 (1981): 67-81.

299.   Kandel, R. F., and Heider, M. "Friendship and Factionalism in a Tri-ethnic Housing Complex for the Elderly in North Miami." *Anthropological Quarterly*, 52, no. 1 (1979): 49-59. See also: Housing.

300.   Keller, J. B. "Volunteer Activities for Ethnic Minority Elderly." In *Retirement: Concepts and Realities*, ed. by E. P. Stanford. San Diego: San Diego State University, 1978.

301.   Langston, E. "The Role and Value of Natural Support Systems in Retirement." In *Retirement: Concepts and Realities*, ed. by E. P. Stanford. San Diego: San Diego State University, 1978. See also: Work and Retirement; Mental Health and Life Satisfaction.

302.   _____. "Community Involvement and Research." In *Minority Aging Research: Old Issues—New Approaches*, ed. by E. P. Stanford. San Diego: San Diego State University, 1979. See also: Theory, Research, and Training.

303.   McFadden, M. B. "An Empirical Examination of New and Meaningful Community Roles for the Minority Retiree." In *Minority Aging: Policy Issues for the '80's*, ed. by E. P. Stanford. San Diego: San Diego State University, 1980. See also: Work and Retirement; Theory, Research, and Training.

304.   Pritchard, D. C. "Personal and Social Supportive Services: New and Meaningful Role Opportunities." In *Minority Aging: Policy Issues for the '80's*, ed. by E. P. Stanford. San Diego: San Diego State University, 1980. See also: Support Services and Service Delivery.

Social Policy and Politics

305.   Bechill, W. "Politics of Aging and Ethnicity." In *Ethnicity and Aging: Theory Research and Policy*, ed. by D. E. Gelfand and A. J. Kutzik. New York: Springer Publishing Co., 1979.

306.   Benedict, R. "Federal Policies and the Minority Elderly." In *Retirement: Concepts and Realities*, ed. by E. P. Stanford. San Diego: San Diego State University, 1978.

307. Bengtson, V. L.; Moore, S. F.; Simic, A.; Abarbanely, J.; and Velez, I. C. "Social and Cultural Contexts of Aging: Implications for Social Policy." In *Cross Cultural Perspectives on Aging*. Los Angeles: The Ethel Percy Andrus Gerontology Center, University of Southern California, 1977.

308. Binstock, R. H. "Interest-Group Liberalism and the Politics of Aging." *Gerontologist*, 1 (1972): 265-79.

309. Cantor, M. "Neighbors and Friends: An Overlooked Resource in the Informal Support System." *Research on Aging*, 1 (1979): 434-63.

310. Chacon, P. "Strategies for Affecting Legislative Priorities." In *Minority Aging and the Legislative Process: Third Institute Proceedings*, ed. by E. P. Stanford. San Diego: San Diego State University, 1977.

311. Chino, W. E. "A Historical Perspective of the National Council on Aging." Billings, Montana: Second National Indian Conference on Aging, 1978.

312. Cottin, L. "Elders: The Minorities." In *Elders in Rebellion: A Guide to Senior Activism*. New York: Doubleday, 1979.

313. Cuellar, J. B.; Stanford, E. P.; and Miller-Soule, D. I. "A Human Service Model: Future Directions for Aging Policy and Minorities." In *Understanding Minority Aging: Perspectives and Sources*, ed. by J. B. Cuellar, E. P. Stanford, and D. I. Miller-Soule. San Diego: San Diego State University, 1982.

314. Cuellar, J. B.; Weeks, J.; Jackson-Nelson, J. R.; and Dixon, J. *Minority Elderly Americans: A Prototype for Area Agencies on Aging*. San Diego: Allied Home Health Association, 1980.

315. Dominguez, R. "Political Considerations for Change." In *Minority Aging and the Legislative Process: Third Institute Proceedings*, ed. by E. P. Stanford. San Diego: San Diego State University, 1977.

316. Federal Council on Aging. *Policy Issues Concerning the Elderly Minorities: A Staff Report*. Washington, D.C.: U.S. Government Printing Office, 1979.

317. _____. "Policy Issues Concerning the Elderly Minorities." Washington, D.C.: U.S. Government Printing Office, 1979.

318. Gold, B. "The Role of the Federal Government in the Provision of Social Services to Older Persons." *Annals of the American Academy of Political and Social Science*, 415 (September 1974): 55-69. See also: Support Services and Service Delivery.

319.   Heimstra, S. "Legislative Procedures and Your Input." In *Minority Aging: Third Institute on Minority Aging Proceedings*, ed. by E. P. Stanford. San Diego: San Diego State University, 1977.

320.   Human Resources Corporation. *Policy Issues Concerning the Minority Elderly*. San Francisco, 1978.

321.   Jackson, H. C. "National Goals and Priorities in the Social Welfare of the Aging." *Gerontologist*, *11*, no. 4 (1971): 88-94.

322.   Jamison, J. "Overview of Policy Issues and Their Impact on the Ethnic Elderly." In *Minority Aging and the Legislative Process: Third Institute Proceedings*, ed. by E. P. Stanford. San Diego: San Diego State University, 1977.

323.   _____. "Strategies for Effective Input by the Elderly." In *Minority Aging and the Legislative Process: Third Institute Proceedings*, ed. by E. P. Stanford. San Diego: San Diego State University, 1977.

324.   Kamikawa, L. "An Uphill Road: Minorities and Private Sector Funding." *Generations*, *7*, no. 4 (1983): 26-27, 65.

325.   Kerschner, P. A., ed. *Advocacy and Age: Issues, Experiences, Strategies*. Los Angeles: University of Southern California Press, 1976.

326.   Kutzik, A. J. "American Social Provision for the Aged: An Historical Perspective." In *Ethnicity and Aging: Theory, Research, and Policy*, ed. by D. E. Gelfand and A. J. Kutzik. New York: Springer, 1979.

327.   Lambrinos, J. J., and Torres-Gil, F. "Policymakers Historically Ignore Minorities." *Generations* (May 1980): 24-72.

328.   Langston, E. J. "Policy Impact on Training and Aging Curriculums." In *Minority Aging Research: Old Issues – New Approaches*, ed. by E. P. Stanford. San Diego: San Diego State University, 1979. See also: Education; Theory, Research, and Training.

329.   Leslie, F. R. "Policy and the Minority Aged at the State Level." In *Minority Aging and the Legislative Process: Third Institute Proceedings*, ed. by E. P. Stanford. San Diego: San Diego State University, 1977.

330.   Levy, J. "Historical and Current Perspectives of Legislation." In *Minority Aging and the Legislative Process: Third Institute Proceedings*, ed. by E. P. Stanford. San Diego: San Diego State University, 1977.

331.   _____. "Legislative Concern for Ethnic Aging." In *Minority Aging*, ed. by E. P. Stanford. San Diego: San Diego State University, 1975.

332. Meyers, A. "Ethnicity and Aging: Public Policy and Ethnic Differences in Aging and Old Age." In *Public Policies for an Aging Population*, ed. by E. Markson and G. Batra. Lexington, Mass.: Lexington Books, 1980.

333. Moriwaki, S. Y. "Research and its Relation to Policy Formulation." In *Minority Aging and the Legislative Process: Third Institute Proceedings*, ed. by E. P. Stanford. San Diego: San Diego State University, 1977. See also: Theory, Research, and Training.

334. Nielson, S. "The State Office on Aging and Legislative Implications." In *Minority Aging and the Legislative Process: Third Institute Proceedings*, ed. by E. P. Stanford. San Diego: San Diego State University, 1977.

335. Raya, A. "Social Policy and the Minority Aging." In *Minority Aging: Institute on Minority Aging Proceedings*, ed. by E. P. Stanford. San Diego: San Diego State University, 1974.

336. Rosenblum, M. J. "Hard Times Hit the Old Hardest." *Social Policy*, 7, no. 3 (1976): 43-47.

337. Schween, R. "Role of the Regional Office." In *Minority Aging and the Legislative Process: Third Institute Proceedings*, ed. by E. P. Stanford. San Diego: San Diego State University, 1977.

338. Serow, W. J. "Considerations on the Present and Future Wellbeing of Older Americans." In *Minority Aging: Policy Issues for the '80's*, ed. by E. P. Stanford. San Diego: San Diego State University, 1980.

339. Snyder, D. C. "Social Policy and Economic Status: Reducing Income Differences Between Elderly Whites and Nonwhites." In *Minority Aging: Sociological and Social Psychological Issues*, ed. by R. C. Manuel. Westport, Conn.: Greenwood Press, 1982.

340. Solomon, B. "Minority Group Issues and Benefit Programs for the Elderly—Groundwork Paper 2." In *Policy Issues Concerning the Minority Elderly: Final Report, Six Papers*. San Francisco: Human Resources Corporation, 1978.

341. Sotomayor, M. "Considerations and Implications for Policy Analysis." In *Minority Aging*, ed. by E. P. Stanford. San Diego: San Diego State University, 1975.

342. Stanford, E. P., ed. *Minority Aging and the Legislative Process.* San Diego: San Diego State University, 1977.

343. Stanford, E. P. "Non-Chronological Definitions of Aging: Policy Implications." *Generations* (Summer 1977): 16-17. See also: Theory, Research, and Training.

344.   Torres-Gil, F. "The Special Interest Concerns of the Minority Profes-
       sional: An Evolutionary Process in Affecting Social Policies for the
       Minority Aged." In *Minority Aging: Sociological and Social Psychological
       Issues*, ed. by R. C. Manuel. Westport, Conn.: Greenwood Press,
       1982.

345.   _____. "Policy Questions: Federal Agencies Open Doors to
       Minority Participation." *Generations* (Summer 1977): 15.

346.   Torres-Gil, F.; Owens, Y.; and Wolf, R. "The Minority Elderly and
       the Conference." In *The 1971 White House Conference on Aging: An
       Overview of the Conference Activities*. Waltham, Mass.: Brandeis
       University, 1973.

347.   Trela, J. E., and Sokolovsky, J. H. "Culture, Ethnicity, and Policy for
       the Aged." In *Ethnicity and Aging*, ed. by D. E. Gelfand and A. J.
       Kutzik. New York: Springer, 1979.

348.   U.S. Department, Health, Education, and Welfare. *Older Americans'
       Act of 1965, as Amended: History and Related Acts*. Washington, D.C.:
       U.S. Dept. Health, Education, and Welfare, 1979.

349.   Williams, L. T. "The Legislative Process and the Minority Elderly." In
       Minority Aging: Third Institute on Minority Aging Proceedings, ed. by
       E. P. Stanford. San Diego: San Diego State University, 1977.

350.   Yip, B. C. "Policy Impact of Minority Aging Research on the Com-
       munity." In *Minority Aging Research: Old Issues – New Approaches*, ed.
       by E. P. Stanford. San Diego: San Diego State University, 1979.

Social Security and Old Age Assistance

351.   Bell, D. "Proposed Changes in Social Security." In *Minority Aging
       Research: Old Issues – New Approaches*, ed. by   E. P. Stanford. San
       Diego: San Diego State University, 1979.

352.   Chase, J. W. "Social Security and Supplemental Income." In *Minority
       Aging and the Legislative Process: Third Institute Proceedings*, ed. by E. P.
       Stanford. San Diego: San Diego State University, 1977.

353.   Davis, K. "Equal Treatment and Unequal Benefits: The Medicine
       Program." *Milbank Memorial Fund Quarterly*, 53, no. 4 (1975): 449-88.
       See also: Prejudice, Discrimination, Racism, and Stereotyping.

354.   England, L. "Is There Justification for Full Social Security Benefits at
       an Earlier Age? In *Minority Aging: Policy Issues for the '80's*, ed. by E. P.
       Stanford. San Diego: San Diego State University, 1980.

355.   "Reports on the 1979 Advisory Council on Social Security." *Social Security Bulletin*, *43*, no. 1 (1980): 3-15.

Support Services and Service Delivery

356.   Adams, J. P. "Service Arrangements Preferred by Minority Elderly—A Cross-Cultural Survey." *Journal of Gerontological Social Work*, *3*, no. 2 (1980): 39-57.

357.   Amor, C. "Multi-Cultures, Varied Programming." *Generations* (Summer 1977): 20.

358.   Anderson, F. E. "Program Innovation for New and Meaningful Roles for Minority Elderly Persons." In *Minority Aging: Policy Issues for the '80's*, ed. by E. P. Stanford. San Diego: San Diego State University, 1980.

359.   Barg, S., and Hirsch, C. "A Successor Model for Community Support of Low-Income, Minority Group Aged." *Aging and Human Development*, *3* (1972): 243-51. See also: Demographic and Socioeconomic Characteristics.

360.   Bell, D.; Kasschau, P.; and Zellman, G. *Delivery Services to Elderly Members of Minority Groups: A Critical Review of the Literature*. Santa Monica: Rand Corporation, 1976.

361.   Bell, D., and Zellman, G. *Issues in Services Delivery to Ethnic Elderly*. Santa Monica: Rand Corporation, 1976.

362.   Berkman, B., and Rehr, H. "The Search for Early Indicators of Social Service Needs Among Elderly Hospital Patients." *Journal of the American Geriatrics Society*, *22* (1974): 416-21.

363.   Brody, S.; Finkle, H.; and Hirsch, C. "Benefit Alert: Outreach Program for the Aged." *Social Work 17*, no. 1 (1972): 14-23.

364.   Carp, F. M. "Use of Community Resources and Social Adjustment of the Elderly." In *Proceedings of Seminars, 1965-1969*. Durham: Duke University, 1969. See also: Mental Health and Life Satisfaction.

365.   Colen, J. N. "Using Natural Helping Networks in Social Service Delivery Systems." In *Minority Aging: Sociological and Social Psychological Issues*, ed. by R. C. Manuel. Westport, Conn.: Greenwood Press, 1982.

366.   Cortez, T. "Will an Increase in Accessibility Result in an Increase in Utilization of Services?" In *Minority Aging: Policy Issues for the '80's*, ed. by E. P. Stanford. San Diego: San Diego State University, 1980.

367. Cuellar, J. "Understanding Culture for the Delivery of Services to Minority Elders." In *Black/Chicano Elderly: Service Delivery Within a Cultural Context*, ed. by R. Wright, Jr. Arlington Graduate School of Social Work, University of Texas at Arlington, 1980.

368. _____. "What is the History of Minority Senior Programs?" *Somos*, 1 (1978): 12-14.

369. Evans, R., and Northwood, L. "The Utility of Locality Based Social Networks." *Journal of Minority Aging*, 3 (1978): 199-211.

370. Fandetti, D. "Ethnicity and Neighborhood Services." In *Reaching People: The Structure of Neighborhood Services*, ed. by D. Thurz and J. Vigilante. Beverly Hills: Sage, 1978.

371. Fields, C. "Service Delivery and Consumer Participation." In *Minority Aging*, ed. by E. P. Stanford. San Diego: San Diego State University, 1974.

372. Gallego, D. T. "To Provide or Not to Provide Services for Minority Elderly . . . . That is the Question." In *Minority Aging: Policy Issues for the '80's*, ed. by E. P. Stanford. San Diego: San Diego State University, 1980.

373. Guttmann, D. "Perspective on Equitable Share in Public Benefits by Minority Elderly: Executive Summary." Washington, D.C.: Catholic University of America, 1980.

374. Guttmann, D., and Cuellar, J. B. "Barriers to Equitable Service." *Generations*, 6, no. 3 (1982): 31-33.

375. Harbert, A. S., and Ginsberg, L. H. "The Special Problems of Minority, Ethnic, Women, and Rural Elderly." In *Human Services for Older Adults: Concepts and Skills*. Belmont, Calif.: Wadsworth, 1979.

376. Hirsch, C. "Serving Aged Residents of Central City Neighborhoods." In *Challenges Facing Senior Centers in the Nineteen Seventies*, ed. by A. G. Wolfson. New York: National Council on the Aging, 1968.

377. Holmes, D.; Holmes, M.; Steinbach, L.; Hausner, T.; and Rocheleau, B. "The Use of Community-Based Services in Long Term Care by Older Minority Persons." *Gerontologist*, 19, no. 4 (1979): 389-97. See also: Health, Medicine, and Folk Medicine.

378. Hoyt, D., and Babchuk, N. "Ethnicity and the Voluntary Associations of the Aged." *Ethnicity*, 8 (March 1981): 67-81.

379. Ignacio, L. F. "Some Views on Organizing Senior Citizens." In *Comprehensive Service Delivery Systems for the Minority Aged*, ed. by E. P. Stanford. San Diego: San Diego State University, 1977.

380. Jackson, H. C. "Federal Council on the Aging from the Ethnic Minority Perspective." In *Comprehensive Service Delivery Systems for the Minority Aged*, ed. by E. P. Stanford. San Diego: San Diego University, 1977.

381. _____. "Service Delivery Systems—Role of Minority Elderly in Determining Own Destiny." In *Minority Aging: Institute on Minority Aging Proceedings*, ed. by E. P. Stanford. San Diego: San Diego State University, 1974.

382. Jacobson, S. G. "Equity in the Use of Public Benefits by Minority Elderly." In *Minority Aging: Sociological and Social Psychological Issues*, ed. by R. C. Manuel. Westport, Conn.: Greenwood Press, 1982.

383. Kent, D. P. "Changing Welfare to Serve Minority Aged." In *Minority Aged in America—Occasional Papers in Gerontology No. 10*. Ann Arbor: Institute of Gerontology, University of Michigan-Wayne State University, 1973.

384. Kent, P.; Hirsch C.; and Barg, S. "Indigenous Workers as a Crucial Link in the Total Support System for Low-Income, Minority Group Aged: A Report on Innovative Field Technique in Survey Research." *Aging and Human Development*, 2 (1971): 189-96. See also: Demographic and Socioeconomic Characteristics.

385. King, S., and McNeil, J. "Agency Based Planning and Programming for Effective Service Delivery to the Minority Elderly: Guidelines for Increasing Minority Elderly Participation in Human Services Programs." In *Black/Chicano Elderly: Service Delivery Within a Cultural Context*, ed. by R. Wright. Arlington, Texas: Graduate School of Social Work, University of Texas at Arlington, 1980.

386. Law, A. "Home Health Service: An Option for Care of the Elderly Patient." In *Comprehensive Delivery Systems for the Minority Aged*, ed. by E. P. Stanford. San Diego: San Diego State University, 1977.

387. Lawton, M.; Newcomer, R.; Byerts, T., eds. *Community Planning for an Aging Society: Designing Services and Facilities*. Stroudsburg, Pennsylvania: Dowden, Hutchinson, and Ross, 1976.

388. Levy, J. J. "Minority Aging—Services Respond to Their Cultural Needs." In *Comprehensive Service Delivery Systems for the Minority Aged*, ed. by E. P. Stanford. San Diego: San Diego State University, 1977.

389. _____. "State Programs for the Aging—Their Progress Toward Minority Institute Goals." In *Retirement: Concepts and Realities*, ed. by E. P. Stanford. San Diego: San Diego State University, 1978.

390.   Lopata, H. Z. "Support Systems of Elderly Urbanites: Chicago of the
        1970's." *Gerontologist, 15* (1975): 35-41.

391.   Mayer, M.; Engler, M.; and Lewis, B. *Home Delivered Meals Survey
        Second Report: The Support Systems of Participants in Home-Delivered
        Meal Programs in New York City.* New York: New York City Depart-
        ment for the Aging, 1982.

392.   Mayers, R. S. "Self-Help Groups: An Overview." In *Black/Chicano
        Elderly: Service Delivery Within a Cultual Context,* ed. by R. Wright.
        Arlington, Texas: Graduate School of Social Work, University of
        Texas at Arlington, 1980.

393.   Mindel, C. H. "Program Evaluation for Social Services to the
        Minority Elderly." In *Black/Chicano Elderly: Service Delivery Within a
        Cultural Context,* ed. by R. Wright. Arlington, Texas: Graduate
        School of Social Work, Univerity of Texas at Arlington, 1980.

394.   Palmore, E. "Variables Related to Needs Among the Aged Poor."
        Journal of Gerontology, 26 (1971): 524-31.

395.   Ramirez, F. A. "Home Health Care in the Minority Community." In
        Comprehensive Service Delivery Systems for the Minority Aged, ed. by
        E. P. Stanford. San Diego: San Diego State University, 1977. See
        also: Health, Medicine, and Folk Medicine.

396.   Raya, A. E. "Integration of Health and Social Services." In *Com-
        prehensive Service Delivery Systems for the Minority Aged,* ed. by E. P.
        Stanford. San Diego: San Diego State University, 1977. See also:
        Health, Medicine, and Folk Medicine.

397.   Sainer, J. S. *Home Delivered Meals Participants Survey First Report: An
        Overview of Participant Characteristics and Their Relations to Criteria for
        Program Participation.* New York: New York City Department for
        the Aging, 1982. See also: Demographic and Socioeconomic
        Characteristics.

398.   Solomon, B. "Minority Group Issues and Benefit Programs for the
        Elderly – Groundwork Paper 2." In *Policy Issues Concerning the Minor-
        ity Elderly: Final Report, Six Papers.* San Francisco: Human Resources
        Corporation, 1978.

399.   Stanford, E. P., ed. *Comprehensive Service Delivery Systems for Minority
        Aged: Fourth Institute on Minority Aging Proceedings.* San Diego: San
        Diego State University, 1977.

400.   _____. "Perspectives Toward Comprehensive Services for
        Minority Elderly." In *Comprehensive Service Delivery Systems for the
        Minority Aged,* ed. by E. P. Stanford. San Diego: San Diego State
        University, 1977.

401. Taylor, S. P. "Simple Models of Complexity: Pragmatic Considerations in Providing Services for Minority Elderly." In *Minority Aging: Policy Issues for the '80's*, ed. by E. P. Stanford. San Diego: San Diego State University, 1980.

402. U.S. Commission on Civil Rights. *Minority Elderly Services: New Programs, Old Problems, Part I*. Washington, D.C.: U.S. Government Printing Office, 1982.

403. Valle, R. "The Knowledge Base for Planning Services to Minority Elderly – Groundwork Paper 1." In *Policy Issues Concerning the Minority Elderly: Final Report, Six Papers*. San Francisco: Human Resources Corporation, 1978. See also: Social Policy and Politics.

404. Washington, J. "A Day Care Program." In *Minority Aging Research: Old Issues – New Approaches*, ed. by E. P. Stanford. San Diego: San Diego State University, 1979.

405. Wilkins, D. and Fraser, D. *Evaluation of Programs Affecting the Elderly Minority Poor in Selected U.S. Cities*. Vol. 1. New York: Forward Management Associates, 1977. See also: Demographic and Socioeconomic Characteristics.

406. _____. *Evaluation of Programs Affecting the Elderly Minority Poor in Selected U.S. Cities*. Vol. II. New York: Forward Management Associates, 1977. See also: Demographic and Socioeconomic Characteristics.

407. Wolfson, A., ed. *Challenges Facing Senior Centers in the Nineteen Seventies*. New York: National Council on the Aging, 1969.

408. Wong, A. S. "Self-Help for the Elderly." In *Comprehensive Service Delivery Systems for the Minority Aged*, ed. by. E. P. Stanford. San Diego: San Diego State University, 1977.

409. Woolf, L. M. "Serving Minority Persons in a Senior Center." In *Challenges Facing Senior Centers in the Nineteen Seventies*, ed. by A. Wolfson. New York: National Council on the Aging, 1969.

410. Wright, R. "Assessing the Needs of the Minority Aged: Methodologies and Techniques." In *Black/Chicano Elderly: Service Delivery Within A Cultural Context*, ed. by R. Wright. Arlington, Texas: Graduate School of Social Work, University of Texas at Arlington, 1980. See also: Theory, Research, and Training.

411. _____, ed. *Black/Chicano Elderly: Service Delivery Within a Cultural Context*. Arlington, Texas: Graduate School of Social Work, University of Texas at Arlington, 1980.

412.   Yip, B. C. "Home Help Program." In *Comprehensive Service Delivery Systems for the Minority Aged,* ed. by E. P. Stanford. San Diego: San Diego State University, 1977.

Theory, Research, and Training

413.   Anderson, B. G. "The Process of Deculturation–Its Dynamic Among United States Aged." *Anthropological Quarterly, 45* (1972): 209-16.

414.   Arrieta, R. "Developing an Accurate Data Base." In *Minority Aging: Policy Issues for the '80's,* ed. by E. P. Stanford. San Diego: San Diego State University, 1980.

415.   Arth, M. "Aging: A Cross-Cultural Perspective." In *Research Planning and Action for the Elderly: The Power and Potentials of Social Sciences.* New York: Behavioral Pbns., 1972.

416.   Bagley, S. "The National Institute on Aging." In *Minority Aging Research: Old Issues–New Approaches,* ed. by E. P. Stanford. San Diego: San Diego State University, 1979.

417.   Bateson, G. "Cultural Ideas About Aging." In *Research on Aging,* ed. by H. E. Jones. New York: Social Science Research Council, 1950.

418.   Beattie, W. "Curriculum Development Workshop." In *Minority Aging,* ed. by E. P. Stanford. San Diego: San Diego State University, 1974.

419.   Bengtson, V. "Ethnicity and Aging: Problems and Issues in Current Social Science Inquiry." In *Ethnicity and Aging: Theory, Research, and Policy,* ed. by D. E. Gelfand and A. J. Kutzik. New York: Springer, 1979.

420.   _____, ed. *Gerontological Research and Community Concern: A Case Study of a Multidisciplinary Project.* Los Angeles: The Ethel Percy Andrus Gerontology Center, University of Southern California, 1974.

421.   Bengtson, V.; Dowd, J.; Smith, D.; and Inkeles, A. "Modernization, Modernity, and Perceptions of Aging: A Cross-Cultural Study." *Journal of Gerontology, 30,* no. 6 (1975): 688-95.

422.   Bengtson, V.; Grigsby, E.; Corry, E.; and Hruby, M. "Relating Academic Research to Community Concerns: A Case Study in Collaborative Effort." *Journal of Social Issues, 33* (1977): 75-92.

423. Bengtson, V.; Kasschau, P.; and Ragan, P. "The Impact of Social Structure on Aging Individuals." In *Handbook of the Psychology of Aging*, ed. by J. E. Birren and K. W. Schaie. New York: Van Nostrand Reinhold, 1977.

424. Bengtson, V.; Ragan, P.; and McConnell, S. *Social and Cultural Contexts of Aging: Anthropological Report.* Los Angeles: The Ethel Percy Andrus Gerontology Center, University of Southern California, 1977.

425. Biegel, D. E., and Sherman, W. R. "Neighborhood Capacity Building and the Ethnic Aged." In *Ethnicity and Aging: Theory, Research and Aging*, ed. by D. E. Gelfand and A. J. Kutzik. New York: Springer, 1979.

426. Brigham, J. C., and Williamson, N. L. "Cross-Racial Recognition and Age: When You're over 60, Do They Still 'All Look Alike'?" *Personality and Social Psychology Bulletin*, 5, no. 2 (April 1979): 218-22.

427. Brodsky, D. M. "The Conflict Perspective and Understanding Aging Among Minorities." In *Minority Aging: Sociological and Social Psychological Issues*, ed. by R. C. Manuel. Westport, Conn.: Greenwood Press, 1982.

428. Burton, L., and Bengtson, V. L. "Research in Elderly Minority Communities: Problems and Potentials." In *Minority Aging: Sociological and Social Psychological Issues*, ed. by R. C. Manuel. Westport, Conn.: Greenwood Press, 1982.

429. Butler, H.; Habert, A.; and Anderson, F. "Images of the Aging Person: Implications for Research and Practice with Minority Aging." In *Minority Aging: Policy Issues for the '80's*, ed. by E. P. Stanford. San Diego: San Diego State University, 1980.

430. Clark, M. "The Anthropology of Aging: A New Area for Studies of Culture and Personality." *Gerontologist*, 7 (1967): 55-64.

431. _____. "Contributions of Cultural Anthropology to the Study of the Aged." In *Cultural Illness and Health*, ed. by L. Nader and T. L. Maritzki. Washington, D.C.: American Anthropological Association, 1973.

432. Clark, M., and Anderson, B. G. *Culture and Aging: An Anthropological Study of Older Americans.* Springfield, Ill.: Charles C. Thomas, 1967.

433. Cowgill, D. O. "Aging and Modernization: A Revision of the Theory." In *Late Life: Continuities in Environmental Policy*, ed. by J. F. Gubrium. Springfield, Ill.: Charles C. Thomas, 1974.

434. _____. "A Theory of Aging in Cross-Cultural Perspective." In *Aging and Modernization*, ed. by D. O. Cowgill. New York: Appleton-Century-Crofts, 1972.

435. Cuellar, J. B. "Insiders and Outsiders." In *Minority Aging Research: Old Issues – New Approaches*, ed. by E. P. Stanford. San Diego: San Diego State University, 1979.

436. Cuellar, J. B.; Stanford, E. P.; and Miller-Soule, D. I. "Minority Aging Research: History, Trends, and Gaps." In *Understanding Minority Aging: Perspectives and Sources*, ed. by J. B. Cuellar, E. P. Stanford, and D. I. Miller-Soule. San Diego: San Diego State University, 1982.

437. Cumming, E. and Henry, W. *Growing Old: The Process of Disengagement*. New York: Basic Books, 1961.

438. Eisdorfer, C. "Research, Training, Service and Action Concerns about Aging and Aged Persons: An Overview." In *Proceedings of Research Conference on Minority Group Aged in the South, October 1971*, ed. by J. J. Jackson. Durham, North Carolina: Duke University, 1972.

439. Gelfand, D. E., and Kutzik, A. J. "Conclusions: The Continuing Significance of Ethnicity." In *Ethnicity and Aging: Theory, Research and Policy*, ed. by D. E. Gelfand and A. J. Kutzik. New York: Springer, 1979.

440. _____, eds. *Ethnicity and Aging: Theory, Research, and Policy.* New York: Springer, 1979. See also: Social Policy and Politics.

441. Gentry, D. W. *Geropsychology: A Model of Training and Clinical Service*. Cambridge, Mass: Ballinger, 1975.

442. Green, L. "The Ecology of Aging – Or, Who Needs Old People?" In *Minority Aging Research: Old Issues – New Approaches*, ed. by E. P. Stanford. San Diego: San Diego State University, 1979.

443. Gubrium, J. F. *The Myth of the Golden Years: A Socioenvironmental Theory of Aging*. Springfield, Ill.: Charles C. Thomas, 1973.

444. Guttmann, D. "Some Theoretical and Methodological Issues in Research with Minority Elderly." In *Minority Aging Research: Old Issues – New Approaches*, ed. by E. P. Stanford. San Diego: San Diego State University, 1979.

445. Henretta, J., and Campbell, R. T. "Status Attainment and Status Maintenance: A Study of Stratification in Old Age." *American Sociological Review, 41* (1976): 981-92.

446. Holzberg, C. S. "Cultural Gerontology: Towards an Understanding of Ethnicity and Aging." *Journal of the Canadian Ethnological Society*, *1*, no. 1 (1981): 110-22.

447. _____. "Ethnicity and Aging: Anthropological Perspectives on More Than Just the Minority Elderly." *Gerontologist, 22*, no. 3 (1982): 249-57.

448. _____. "Ethnicity and Aging: Rejoinder." *Gerontologist, 22*, no. 6 (1982): 471-72.

449. Jeffries, V., and Ransford, H. *Social Stratification: A Multiple Hierarchy Approach*. Boston: Allyn and Bacon, Inc., 1980.

450. Jones, H. E., ed. *Research on Aging*. New York: Social Science Research Council, 1950.

451. Kiefer, C. W. "Notes on Anthropology and the Minority Elderly." *Gerontologist, 11* (1971): 94-98.

452. Komaroff, A.; Masuda, M.; and Holmes, T. "The Social Readjustment Rating Scale: A Comparative Study of Negro, Mexican and White Americans." *Journal of Psychosomatic Research, 12* (1968): 121-28.

453. Lacayo, C. G. "Research on Anthropology and the Minority Elderly." *Gerontologist, 11* (1971): 94-98.

454. Lipman, A. "Minority Aging from the Exchange and Structure-Functionalist Perspective." In *Minority Aging: Sociological and Social Psychological Issues*, ed. by R. C. Manuel. Westport, Conn.: Greenwood Press, 1982.

455. McClure, J. F., and Arrieta, R. C. "The Operationalization and Transformation of Field Research to Study the Needs and Social Problems of Minority Elderly: A Search for a Conceptual Model." In *Minority Aging Research: Old Issues—New Approaches*, ed. by E. P. Stanford. San Diego: San Diego State University, 1979.

456. McDonald, T. "Is Minority Aging Research Relevant?" In *Minority Aging Research: Old Issues—New Approaches*, ed. by E. P. Stanford. San Diego: San Diego State University, 1979.

457. Manuel, R. C. "The Dimension of Ethnic Minority Identification: An Exploratory Analysis Among Elderly Black Americans." In *Minority Aging: Sociological and Social Psychological Issues*, ed. by R. C. Manuel. Westport, Conn.: Greenwood Press, 1982.

458. _____. "The Minority Aged: Providing a Conceptual Perspective." In *Minority Aging: Sociological and Social Psychological Issues*, ed. by R. C. Manuel. Westport, Conn.: Greenwood Press, 1982.

459. _____. "The Study of the Minority Aged in Historical Perspective." In *Minority Aging: Sociological and Social Psychological Issues*, ed. by R. C. Manuel. Westport, Conn.: Greenwood Press, 1982.

460. _____. "Social Research Among the Minority Aged: Providing a Perspective for a Select Number of Issues." In *Research and Training in Minority Aging*, ed. by G. Sherman. Washington, D. C.: National Center on the Black Aged, 1978.

461. Markides, K. S. "Ethnicity and Aging: A Comment." *Gerontologist*, 22, no. 6 (1982): 467-70.

462. _____. "Ethnicity, Aging and Society: Theoretical Lessons from the United States Experience." *Archives of Gerontology and Geriatrics*. In press.

463. _____. "Methodological Problems in Conducting Research on Minority Aged." In *Black/Chicano Elderly: Service Delivery Within a Cultural Context*, ed. by R. Wright. Arlington: Graduate School of Social Work, University of Texas at Arlington, 1980.

464. Markides, K. S., and Boldt, J. S. "Change in Subjective Age Among the Elderly: A Longitudinal Analysis." *Gerontologist*, 23, no. 4 (1983): 422-27.

465. Maxwell, R., and Silverman, P. "Information and Esteem: Cultural Considerations in the Treatment of Aged." *Aging and Human Development*, 1 (1970): 361-92.

466. Maykovich, M. K. "The Difficulties of Minority Research in Minority Communities," *Journal of Social Issues*, 33, no. 4 (1977): 108-19.

467. Miller, C. "The Impact of Current Research on Future Research." In *Minority Aging Research: Old Issues—New Approaches*, ed. by. E. P. Stanford. San Diego: San Diego State University, 1979.

468. Montero, D. "Research Among Racial and Cultural Minorities: An Overview." *Journal of Social Issues*, 33, no. 4 (1977): 1-10.

469. Montiel, M., and Wong, P. "A Theoretical Critique of the Minority Perspective." *Social Casework*, 64, no. 2 (1983): 112-17.

470. Moore, J. W. "Situational Factors Affecting Minority Aging." *Gerontologist*, 11 (1971): 30-35.

471. Morgan, D. L. "Ethnicity and Aging: Theory, Research, and Policy." *Contemporary Sociology: A Journal of Reviews*, 10, no. 2 (1981): 208-9. See also: Social Policy and Politics.

472. Morgan, H. N., and Bellos, N. S. "The State of the Art of Research: Implications for Curriculum." In *Research and Training in Minority Aging*, ed. by G. Sherman. Washington, D.C.: National Center on the Black Aged, 1978.

473. Moriwaki, S. Y. "Uses and Comparability of Secondary Data: How to Make the Most of What We Have." In *Minority Aging Research: Old Issues—New Approaches*, ed. by E. P. Stanford. San Diego: San Diego State University, 1979.

474. Murase, K. "Research Dissemination and Utilization." In *Minority Aging Research: Old Issues—New Approaches*, ed. by E. P. Stanford. San Diego: San Diego State University, 1979.

475. Palmore, E. "Cross-cultural Research: State of the Art." *Research on Aging*, 5, no. 1 (1983): 45-47.

476. Pierce, R. C.; Clark, M.; and Kaufman, S. "Generation and Ethnic Identity: A Typological Analysis." *International Journal of Aging and Human Development*, 9, no. 1 (1978-79): 19-29.

477. Press, I., and McKool, Jr., M. "Social Structure and Status of the Aged: Toward Some Valid Cross-cultural Generalizations." *Aging and Human Development*, 3, no. 4 (1972): 297-306. [Now known as *International Journal of Aging and Human Development*.]

478. Ragan, P. K. *Aging Among Blacks, Mexican Americans, and Anglos—Problems and Possibilities of Research as Reflected in the Literature.* Los Angeles: The Ethel Percy Andrus Gerontology Center, University of Southern California, 1973.

479. Ragan, P. K., and Bengtson, V. L. *Aging Among Blacks, Mexican Americans and Whites: Development, Procedures and Results of the Community Survey.* Los Angeles: The Ethel Percy Andrus Gerontology Center, University of Southern California, 1977.

480. Rey, A. B. "Activity and Disengagement: Theoretical Orientations in Social Gerontology and Minority Aging." In *Minority Aging: Sociological and Social Psychological Issues*, ed. by R. C. Manuel. Westport, Conn.: Greenwood Press, 1982.

481. Rosow, I. *Social Integration of the Aged.* New York: Free Press, 1967.

482. Schaie, K. W.; Orchowsky, S.; and Parham, I. A. "Measuring Age and Sociocultural Changes: The Case of Race and Life Satisfaction." In *Minority Aging: Sociological and Social Psychological Issues*, ed. by R. C. Manuel. Westport, Conn.: Greenwood Press, 1982. See also: Mental Health and Life Satisfaction.

483. Sherman, G. A., ed. *Curriculum Guidelines in Minority Aging.* Washington, D. C.: The National Center on Black Aged, 1980.

484. Smith, R., et al. "Cultural Differences in the Life Cycle and the Concept of Time." In *Aging and Leisure,* ed. by R. Kleemeir. Oxford: Oxford University Press, 1961.

485. Smith, S. H. "Major Concerns: A Summing Up of Gerontological Research and Training." In *Proceedings of the Research Conference on Minority Group Aged in the South,* ed. by J. J. Jackson. Durham: Duke University, 1972.

486. Solomon, B. B. "Better Planning Through Research." In *Comprehensive Service Delivery Systems for the Minority Aged,* ed. by E. P. Stanford. San Diego: San Diego State University, 1977. See also: Support Services and Service Delivery.

487. Stanford, E. P. "Research as an Essential Tool." In *Minority Aging Research: Old Issues–New Approaches,* ed. by E. P. Stanford. San Diego: San Diego State University, 1979.

488. _____. "Theoretical and Practical Relationships Among Aged Blacks and Other Minorities." *The Black Scholar: Journal of Black Studies, 13,* no. 1 (1982): 49-57.

489. Steinberg, R. M. "Impact of Minority Aging Research on Services for Minority Elderly." In *Minority Aging Research: Old Issues–New Approaches,* ed. by E. P. Stanford. San Diego: San Diego State University, 1979. See also: Support Services and Service Delivery.

490. Steward, G., ed. *Clinical Studies in Cultural Conflict.* New York: Ronald Press, 1958.

491. Tobin, S. "Theory Workshop." In *Minority Aging,* ed. by E. P. Stanford. San Diego: San Diego State University, 1974.

492. Torres-Gil, F. "Research Statement." In *Minority Aging: Fourth Institute on Minority Aging Proceedings,* ed. by E. P. Stanford. San Diego: San Diego State University, 1977.

493. Torres-Gil, F. and Cuellar, J. B. "The Development of Minority Components in Gerontological Programs: A Rationale and Prospectus." In *Research and Training in Minority Aging,* ed. by G. Sherman. Washington, D.C.: National Center on the Black Aged, 1978.

494. Ward, R. A. "The Stability of Racial Differences Across Age Strata." *Sociology and Social Research, 67,* no. 3 (1983): 312-23.

495.   Watson, W. H. "On Ethnic Variations in Aging Behavior: Some Problems for Future Research." In *Gerontology in Higher Education*, ed. by H. Sterns, E. Ansello, B. Sprouse, and R. M. Layfield-Faux. Belmont, California: Wadsworth, 1979.

Transportation

496.   Bengtson, V. L.; Torres-Gil, F.; Newquist, D.; and Simonin, M. *Transportation: The Diverse Aged. Policy Report One, USC Research Program on Social and Cultural Contexts on Aging.* Los Angeles: The Ethel Percy Andrus Gerontology Center, University of Southern California, 1976.

497.   Cornehls, J., and Taebel, D. "The Outsiders and Urban Transportation." *Social Science Journal, 13* (1976): 61-74.

498.   Torres-Gil, F.; Newquist, D.; and Simonin, M. *Transportation: The Diverse Aged.* Washington, D.C.: U.S. Government Printing Office, 1977.

Women

499.   Block, M.; Davidson, J.; and Grambs, J. "Ethnic and Racial Variations in Older Women." In *Women Over Forty: Visions and Realities.* New York: Springer, 1981.

500.   Darrow, S. T. "Life Span Behavior Patterns—Class and Ethnic Variations." In *No Longer Young: The Older Woman in America—Occasional Papers in Gerontology No. 11.* Ann Arbor: Institute of Gerontology, University of Michigan-Wayne State University, 1974. See also: Demographic and Socioeconomic Characteristics.

501.   Hunter, K.; Linn, M.; and Pratt, T. C. "Minority Women's Attitudes About Aging." *Experimental Aging Research, 5,* no. 2 (1979): 95-108.

502.   Kivett, V. R. "Loneliness and the Rural Widow." *Family Coordinator* (1978): 389-94. See also: Rural; Mental Health and Life Satisfaction.

503.   Lesnoff-Caravaglia, G. "The Black Granny and the Soviet Babushka: Commonalities and Contrasts." In *Minority Aging: Sociological and Social Psychological Issues,* ed. by R. C. Manuel. Westport, Conn.: Greenwood Press, 1982. See also: Black Americans: Women; European Origin Ethnic Groups: Women.

504.   Weaver, J. L. *National Health Policy and the Underserved: Ethnic Minorities, Women and the Elderly.* St. Louis: C. V. Mosby, 1976. See also: Health, Medicine, and Folk Medicine; Social Policy and Politics.

505.   Youmans, E. G. "Family Disengagement Among Older Urban and Rural Women." *Journal of Gerontology, 22* (1967): 209-11. See also: Marriage and Family.

Work and Retirement

506.   Arnold, W.; Means, T.; and Mann, J. "The Impact of Mandatory Retirement on Minority Elders." In *Retirement: Concepts and Realities*, ed. by E. P. Stanford. San Diego: San Diego State University, 1978.

507.   DiGennar, J. "The Minority Worker and Age Discrimination." In *Minority Aging Research: Old Issues—New Approaches*, ed. by E. P. Stanford. San Diego: San Diego State University, 1979. See also: Prejudice, Discrimination, Racism, and Stereotyping.

508.   Dixon, J. C. "Retirement Legislation and the Minority Aged." In *Minority Aging and the Legislative Process: Third Institute Proceedings*, ed. by E. P. Stanford. San Diego: San Diego State University, 1977. See also: Social Policy and Politics.

509.   Dudovitz, N., and Miller, B. "Effect of Employment Discrimination on Pension Rights." In *Retirement: Concepts and Realities*, ed. by E. P. Stanford. San Diego: San Diego State University, 1978.

510.   Gibson, R. C. "Race and Sex Differences in Work and Retirement." *Quarterly Contact*. The National Center on the Black Aged, 1982.

511.   Levine, M. "Four Models for Age: Work Policy Research." *Gerontologist, 20*, no. 5 (1980): 561-74.

512.   Meier, E. L. "New ERISA Agency Considered and Pension Issues of Women and Minorities." *Aging and Work, 3*, no. 2 (1980): 135-39. See also: Women.

513.   _____. "Over 65: Expectations and Realities of Work and Retirement." *Industrial Gerontology, 2*, no. 2 (1975): 95-109.

514.   Melson, P. A. "Pre-Retirement Planning: Leisure Lifestyle Development." In *Retirement: Concepts and Realities*, ed. by E. P. Stanford. San Diego: San Diego State University, 1978.

515.   National Council on the Aging. *Employment Prospects for Aged Blacks, Chicanos, and Indians*. Washington, D.C.: National Council on the Aging, 1971.

516.   Parashis, C. L. "Employment Program Crosses Cultural Barriers." *Generations* (Summer 1977): 21.

517. Rhodes, L. "Mandatory Retirement Policies: Impact on Income Maintenance for Minority Elders." In *Retirement: Concepts and Realities,* ed. by E. P. Stanford. San Diego: San Diego State University, 1978.

518. _____. "Retirement, Economics, and the Minority Aged." In *Minority Aging: Sociological and Social Psychological Issues,* ed. by R. C. Manuel. Westport, Conn.: Greenwood Press, 1982.

519. Richardson, R. T. "Older Minority Workers: Gloomy Picture Gets Worse." *Generations,* 6, no. 4 (1982): 24, 73.

520. Stanford, E. P. "Perspectives on Ethnic Elderly Retirement." In *Retirement: Concepts and Realities,* ed. by E. P. Stanford. San Diego: San Diego State University, 1978.

521. _____, ed. *Retirement: Concepts and Realities.* San Diego, San Diego State University, 1978.

522. U.S. Department of Labor, Employment and Training Administration. *Employment-Related Problems of Older Workers: A Research Strategy.* R. and D. Monograph 73, U.S. Department of Labor Employment and Training Administration. Washington, D.C.: U.S. Government Printing Office, 1979.

II. BLACK AMERICANS

Crime, Prisons, and the Legal System

523. Ham, J. "The Aged and Aging Black Prison Inmate: An Inquiry into Some Mental Health Consequences of Imprisonment." In *Health and the Black Aged: Proceedings of a Research Symposium.* ed. by W. Watson, J. Skinner, I. Lewis, S. Wesley, B. Allen. Washington D.C.: National Center on Black Aged, 1977. See also: Mental Health and Life Satisfaction.

524. McAdoo, J. L. "Well-Being and Fear of Crime Among the Black Elderly." In *Ethnicity and Aging: Theory, Research, and Policy,* ed. by D. E. Gelfand and A. J. Kutzik. New York: Springer, 1979.

525. Wilty, C. J. "Fear of Crime, Criminal Victimization and Elderly Blacks." *Phylon, 43,* no. 4 (1982): 283-94.

Death and Dying

526. Hawley, I. B. "Death and Dying." In *Proceedings of the Workshop Series on the Black Aged and Aging and the Conference on the Black Aged and Aging,* ed. by J. Dorsett-Robinson. Carbondale: Southern Illinois University, 1974.

527. Jackson, J. J. "Death Rates of Aged Blacks and Whites, United States, 1964-1978." *Black Scholar, 13* (January-February 1982): 36-48.

528. Jackson, M. "The Black Experience with Death." *Omega, 3* (1972): 203-10.

529. Kalish, R. A. "Death and Dying: A Cross-cultural View." In *Proceedings of the Black Aged in the Future,* ed. by J. J. Jackson. Durham: Duke University, 1973.

530. Lipman, A., and Marden, P. "Preparation for Death in Old Age." *Journal of Gerontology, 21* (1966): 426-31.

531. Masamba, J., and Kalish, R. "Death and Bereavement: The Role of the Black Church." *Omega, 7* (1976): 23-24. See also: Religion.

532. McDonald, M. "The Management of Grief: A Study of Black Funeral Practices." *Omega, 4* (1973): 139-48.

533. Peck, D. L. "Official Documentation of the Black Suicide Experience." *Omega, 14,* no. 1 (1983-84): 21-31.

534. Seiden, R. "Mellowing with Age: Factors Influencing the Nonwhite Suicide Rate." *International Journal of Aging and Human Development, 13,* no. 4 (1981): 265-84.

See also 6.

Demographic and Socioeconomic Characteristics

535.   Abbott, J. "Socioeconomic Characteristics of the Elderly: Some Black-White Differences." *Social Security Bulletin, 40* (1977): 16-42. See also: Work and Retirement.

536.   Administration on Aging. "Characteristics of the Black Elderly." Washington, D.C.: U.S. Government Printing Office, 1980. *Statistical Reports on Older Americans,* no. 5.

537.   Alston, J. P., and Knapp, M. J. "Intergenerational Mobility Among Black Americans." *Journal of Black Studies, 4* (1974): 285-302.

538.   Bourg, C. J. "A Social Profile of Black Aged in a Southern Metropolitan Area." In *Proceedings of the Research Conference on Minority Group Aged in the South,* ed. by J. J. Jackson. Durham: Duke University, 1972.

539.   Brotman, H. B. *Facts and Figures on Older Americans.* Washington, D.C.: Administration on Aging, no. 5, 1972.

540.   _____. *Facts and Figures on Older Americans: State Trends, 1960-1970.* Washington, D.C.: Administration on Aging, no. 6, 1974.

541.   Ehrlich, I. F. "Toward a Social Profile on the Aged Black Population in the United States." *International Journal of Aging and Human Development, 4* (1973): 271-76.

542.   Goldstein, S. "Negro-White Differentials in Consumer Problems of the Aged." *Gerontologist, 11* (1971): 242-49.

543.   Hill, R. "A Demographic Profile on the Black Elderly." In *Aging* (Sept.-Oct. 1978): 287-88.

544.   _____. "A Profile of the Black Aged." In *Minority Aged in America—Occasional Papers in Gerontology No. 10.* Ann Arbor: Institute of Gerontology, University of Michigan-Wayne State University, 1973.

545.   Hirsch, C. "A Review of Findings on Social and Economic Conditions of Low-Income Black and White Aged of Philadelphia." In *Proceedings of the Research Conference on Minority Group Aged in the South,* ed. by J. J. Jackson. Durham: Duke University, 1972.

546.   Hirsch, C.; Kent, D. P.; and Silverman, S. L. "Homogeneity and Heterogeneity among Low-Income Negro and White Aged." In *Research Planning and Action for the Elderly: The Power and Potentials of Social Science.* New York: Behavioral Pubns., 1972.

547. Hoffman, S. "Black-White Earnings Differentials Over the Life Cycle." In *Five Thousand American Families – Patterns of Economic Progress,* ed by G. J. Duncan and J. N. Morgan. Vol. VI. Ann Arbor: Survey Research Center, University of Michigan, 1978.

548. Hudson, G. H. "Social and Economic Problems Facing the Black Elderly." *Share, 3,* no. 2 (1975): 1-6.

549. Jackson, J. J. "Letter." In *Economics of Aging: Toward a Full Share in Abundance.* Hearing before the Special Committee on Aging, U.S. Senate, Part I, Survey Hearing, Apr. 29-30, 1969. Washington, D.C.: U.S. Government Printing Office, 1969.

550. _____. "Social Stratification of Aged Blacks and Implications for Training Professionals." In *Proceedings of Black Aged in the Future,* ed. by J. J. Jackson. Durham: Duke University, 1973. See also: Theory, Research and Training; Demographic and Socioeconomic Characteristics.

551. Jackson, M.; Kolody, B; and Wood, J. L. "To Be Old and Black: The Case for Double Jeopardy on Income and Health." In *Minority Aging: Sociological and Social Psychological Issues,* ed. by R. C. Manuel. Westport, Conn.: Greenwood Press, 1982.

552. Jenkins, M. M. "Age and Migration Factors in the Socioeconomic Conditions of Urban Blacks and Urban White Women." *Industrial Gerontology,* 9 (1971): 13-17. See also: Women.

553. Kent, D. P. *Social, Economic and Health Conditions of Negro and White Aged and Their Utilization of Community Resources.* University Park: Pennsylvania State University, Department of Sociology, 1971. See also: Health, Medicine, and Folk Medicine; Support Services and Service Delivery.

554. Kivi, R. E., et al., eds. *Michigan Aging Citizens: Characteristics, Opinions, and Service Utilization Patterns.* Ann Arbor: University of Michigan-Wayne State University, 1975. See also: Support Services, and Service Delivery.

555. Liebow, E. *Tally's Corner: A Study of Negro Streetcorner Men.* Boston: Little, Brown, 1967.

556. National Center on the Black Aged. "The Black Aged: Facts and Figures." *NCBA Technical Bulletin Series, 1,* no. 8 (1973).

557. _____. "Thirty-Seven Percent of Black Aged in Poverty in 1973." *NCBA Technical Bulletin Series, 3* (June 1975).

558. Orshansky, M. "The Aged Negro and His Income." *Social Security Bulletin, 27* (Feb. 1964): 3-13.

559. Rubin, L. "Economic Status of Black Persons: Findings from a Survey of Newly Entitled Beneficiaries." *Social Security Bulletin* (Sept. 1974): 16-35. See also: Work and Retirement.

560. Sheppard, H. L. "Age and Migration Factors in the Socio-Economic Condition of Urban Black and White Women." In *New Perspectives on Older Workers.* Upjohn Institute, 1971. See also: Women.

561. Sterne, R. S.; Phillips, J. E.; and Rabushka, A. *The Urban Elderly Poor: Racial and Bureaucratic Conflict.* Lexington, Mass: Lexington Books, 1974. See also: Social Policy and Politics.

562. Taylor, R. J. and Taylor, W. H. "The Social and Economic Status of the Black Elderly." *Phylon*, *43*, no. 4 (1982): 295-306.

563. Tucker, C. J. "Changes in Age Composition of the Rural Black Population of the South from 1950 to 1970." *Phylon*, *36* (1974): 268-75. See also: Rural.

564. U.S. Bureau of the Census. "Characteristic of Households Purchasing Food Stamps." *Current Population Reports*, Series P-23, #6. Washington, D.C.: U.S. Government Printing Office, 1976.

565. _____. "The Social and Economic Status of the Black Population in the United States 1974." Series P-23, #54. Washington, D.C.: U.S. Government Printing Office, 1975.

566. _____. *Negro Population in the United States, 1790-1915.* Westport, Conn.: Greenwood Press, 1969.

567. _____. *Negroes in the United States, 1920-32,* Westport, Conn.: Greenwood Press, 1969.

568. U.S. Department of Human Services. "Characteristics of the Black Elderly – 1980, Statistics Reports on Older Americans." Publication no. (OHDS) 80-20057. Washington, D.C.: Department of Health and Human Services, 1980.

569. Whittington, F. "Aging and the Relative Income Status of Blacks." *Black Aging*, *1* (1975): 6-13.

570. Williams, B. S. "Characteristics of the Black Elderly." Washington, D.C.: Department of HEW, 1980.
See also 30.

Food and Nutrition

571. Boykin, L. S. "Soul Foods for Some Older Americans." *Journal of the American Geriatric Society*, 23 (1975): 380-82.

572. Morris, H. M. "Nutrition for the Aged." In *Proceedings of the Workshop Series on the Black Aging and Aged and the Conference on the Black Aging and Aged,* ed. by J. Dorsett-Robinson. Carbondale: Southern Illinois University, 1974.

573. Nichols, G. J. "Drugs and Nutrition." *Journal of the National Medical Association,* 70, no. 10 (1978): 737-38. See also: Health, Medicine, and Folk Medicine.

574. Ostfeld, A. M. "Nutrition and Aging—Discussant's Perspective." In *Epidemiology of Aging,* ed. by A. M. Ostfeld and D. C. Gibson. Washington, D.C.: U.S. Government Printing Office, no date given, #75-711. See also: Health, Medicine, and Folk Medicine.

575. Ramsey, Jr., E., "Nutritional Research Training and Services Relative to Aging and Aged Blacks." In *Proceedings of Research Conference on Minority Group Aged in the South,* ed by J. J. Jackson. Durham: Duke University, 1972. See also: Theory, Research, and Training.

576. Shank, R. E. "Nutrition and Aging." In *Epidemiology of Aging,* ed. by A. M. Ostfeld and D. C. Gibson. Washington, D.C.: U.S. Government Printing Office, no date given, #75-711. See also: Health, Medicine, and Folk Medicine.

577. Tiven, M. B. "Life Styles and Nutrient Intake in the Elderly." In *Nutrition and Aging,* ed. by M. Winick. New York: John Wiley and Sons, Inc., 1976. See also: Health, Medicine, and Folk Medicine.

General

578. Bardo, H. R. "Attitudes of the Black Aging." In *Proceedings of the Workshop Series on the Black Aged and Aging,* ed. by J. Dorsett-Robinson. Carbondale: Southern Illinois University, 1974.

579. Bild, B., and Havighurst, R. "Senior Citizens in Great Cities: The Case of Chicago." *Gerontologist,* 16, no. 1, part 2 (1976): 1-88.

580. Chang, P., ed. *Readings in Black Aged.* New York: MSS Information Corporation, 1977.

581. Davis, D. "Growing Old Black." In *Social Problems of the Aging: Readings,* ed. by M. Seltzer, S. Corbett, and R. Atchley. Belmont, California: Wadsworth, 1978.

582. Dorsett-Robinson, J., ed. *Proceedings of the Workshop Series on the Black Aged and Aging and the Conference on the Black Aged and Aging.* Carbondale: Southern Illinois University, 1974.

583. Drake, S. C., and Cayton, H. R. *Black Metropolis: A Study of Negro Life in a Northern City* [Chicago]. New York: Harcourt, Brace & Co., 1945.

584. Eaglin, J. P. "The Nation's Black Elders: This is Not Progress." *Generations*, 6, no. 3 (1982): 29-30, 54.

585. Ehrlich, I. F. "The Aged Black in America: The Forgotten Person." *Journal of Negro Education*, 44, no. 1 (1975): 12-23.

586. Faulkner, A. O.; Heisel, M.; Geismar, S.; and Holbrook, W. *When I was Comin' Up: An Oral History of Aged Blacks*. Hamden, Conn.: Archon, 1982.

587. Ford, J. "Black Aged in the Future in a Predominantly Black Southern Town." In *Proceedings of Black Aged in the Future*, ed. by J. J. Jackson. Durham: Duke University, 1973.

588. Golden, H. M. "Black Ageism." *Social Policy*, 7 (1976): 40-42.

589. Haley, A. "Haley's Rx: Talk, Write, Reunite." *Time*, 14 February 1977: 72.

590. Hicks, N. "Life After 65." *Black Enterprise* (May 1977): 18-22.

591. Hudson, G. H. "The Black Aged: Some Reflections by a Layman." In *Proceedings of the Workshop Series on the Black Aging and Aged and the Conference on the Black Aged and Aging*, ed. by J. Dorsett-Robinson. Carbondale: Southern Illinois University, 1974.

592. _____. "Some Special Problems of Older Black Americans." *Crisis*, 83, no. 3 (1976): 88-90.

593. Jackson, J. J. "Black Aged: In Quest of the Phoenix." In *Triple Jeopardy: Myth or Reality?* Washington, D.C.: National Council on the Aging, 1972. See also: Prejudice, Discrimination, Racism, and Stereotyping.

594. _____. "The Blacklands of Gerontology." *Aging and Human Development*, 2 (1971): 156-71.

595. _____. "Negro Aged in North Carolina." *North Carolina Journal of Mental Health*, 4, no. 1 (1970): 43-52.

596. _____. "Selected Statistical Data on Aging and Aged Blacks." In *Proceedings of the Research Conference on Minority Group Aged in the South*, ed. by J. J. Jackson. Durham: Duke University, 1972. See also: Demographic and Socioeconomic Characteristics.

597. _____, ed. *Proceedings of Black Aged in the Future*. Durham: Duke University, 1973.

598. _____, ed. *Proceedings of Research Conference on Minority Group Aged in the South*. Durham: Duke University, 1972.

599.   Jackson, J. J., and Walls, B. F. "Myths and Realities About Aged
       Blacks." In *Readings in Gerontology*, ed. by M. Brown. St. Louis:
       C. V. Mosby, 1978. See also: Demographic and Socioeconomic
       Characteristics.

600.   Jackson, M., and Wood, J. L. *Aging in America: Implications of the
       Black Aged*. Washington, D.C.: National Council on the Aging,
       1976. See also: General.

601.   James, N. L. "Cultural Differences." In *Proceedings of the Workshop
       Series on the Black Aged and Aging and the Conference on the Black Aged
       and Aging*, ed. by J. Dorsett-Robinson. Carbondale: Southern Illinois
       University, 1974.

602.   Kastenbaum, R., ed. "A Special Issue—Black Aging." *Aging and
       Human Development*, 2, no. 2 (1971): 155-231.

603.   Lacklen, C. "Aged, Black, and Poor: Three Case Studies." *Aging and
       Human Development*, 2 (1971): 202-7. See also: Socioeconomic
       Characteristics.

604.   Marshall, M. "Differential Use of Time." *Workshop on Community Ser-
       vices and the Black Elderly*, ed. by R. H. Davis. Los Angeles: The Ethel
       Percy Andrus Gerontology Center, University of Southern Cali-
       fornia, 1972.

605.   Messer, M. "Race Differences in Selected Attitudinal Dimensions of
       the Elderly." *Gerontologist*, 8 (1968): 245-49.

606.   Miller, K. S., and Dreger, R. M., eds. *Comparative Studies of Blacks
       and Whites in the United States*. New York: Seminar Press, 1973.

607.   Morse, D. W. "Aging in the Ghetto: Themes Expressed by Older
       Black Men and Women Living in a Northern Industrial City." *Indus-
       trial Gerontology*, 3 (1976): 1-10. See also: Women.

608.   National Caucus on the Black Aged. *National Caucus on the Black
       Elderly*. Washington, D.C.: National Caucus, #55, 1971.

609.   _____. *Proceedings of the National Conference on the Black Elderly*.
       Washington, D.C.: National Caucus on the Black Aged, 1971.

610.   New York City Department of the Aging. *The Elderly in the Inner
       City*. New York: New York State Seminar on the Black Aged, 1974.

611.   Palm, C. H. "The Future of the Black Aged in America." In *Pro-
       ceedings of the Black Aged in the Future*, ed. by J. J. Jackson. Durham:
       Duke University, 1973.

612. Register, J. C. "Aging and Race: A Black-White Comparative Analysis." *Gerontologist, 21*, no. 4 (1981): 438-43.

613. Rice, C. "Old and Black." *Harvest Years, 8* (1968): 34-35.

614. Rowan, C. T. *Just Between Us Blacks.* New York: Random House, 1974.

615. Smith, B. K. *Aging in America.* Boston: Beacon, 1973.

616. Solomon, B. "The Black Aged: A Status Report." In *Policy Issues Concerning the Minority Elderly: Final Report, Six Papers.* San Francisco: Human Resources Corporation, 1978. See also: Social Policy and Politics.

617. Stanford, E. P. *The Elder Black.* San Diego: San Diego State University, 1978.

618. Thune, J. M. *Group Portraits in Black and White.* Nashville: Senior Citizens, Inc., 1969.

619. Wylie, F. "Attitudes Toward Aging and the Aged Among Black Americans: South Historical Perspectives." *Aging and Human Development. 2* (1971): 66-70.
See also 55, 91.

Health, Medicine and Folk Medicine

620. Applewhite, H. "Blacks in Public Health." *Journal of the National Medical Association, 66* (1974): 505-10.

621. Baer, H. A. "Towards a Systematic Typology of Black Folk Healers." *Phylon, 43*, no. 4 (1982): 327-43.

622. Bailey, L.; Davis, C.; et al. "Folacin and Iron Status and Hematological Findings in Predominately Black Elderly Persons from Urban Low-Income Households." *American Journal of Clinical Nutrition, 32* (1979): 2346-53.

623. Blake, J. H. "Doctor Can't Do Me No Good: Social Concomitants of Health Care Attitudes and Practices Among Elderly Blacks in Isolated Rural Populations." In *Health and the Black Aged: Proceedings of a Research Symposium,* ed. by W. Watson, J. Skinner, I. Lewis, S. Wesley, and B. Allen. Washington, D.C.: National Center on Black Aged, 1977. See also: Rural.

624. Calloway, N. O. "Medical Aspects of the Aging American Black." In *Proceedings of Black Aged in the Future,* ed. by J. J. Jackson. Durham: Duke University, 1973.

625. Chen, M., and Evans W. "A Study of the Health Status of the Black Population in Alameda County, California." *Medical Care, 16* (1978): 598-603.

626. Dischinger, P.; McDonagh, H.; and Hames, C. "Blood Fibrinolytic Activity, Social Class and Habitual Physical Activity—I. A Study of Black and White Men in Evans County, Georgia." *Journal of Chronic Diseases, 33* (1980): 283-90. See also: Demographic and Socioeconomic Characteristics.

627. German, P. S.; Shapiro, S.; Chase, G. A.; and Vollmer, M. H. "Health Care of the Elderly in a Changing Inner City Community." *Black Aging, 3* (1978): 122-32.

628. Greene, D. R. "Health Indicators and Life Expectancy of the Black Aged: Policy Implications." In *Health and the Black Aged: Proceedings of a Research Symposium*, ed. by W. Watson, J. Skinner, I. Lewis, S. Wesley and B. Allen. Washington, D.C.: National Center on Black Aged, 1977. See also: Mortality; Social Policy and Politics.

629. Harper, B. "Physical and Mental Health Services." In *Community Services and the Black Elderly*, ed. by R. H. Davis. Los Angeles: The Ethel Percy Andrus Gerontology Center, University of Southern California, 1972. See also: Mental Health and Life Satisfaction.

630. Hawkins, R. "Dental Health of Aged Blacks." In *Proceedings of the Black Aged in the Future*, ed. by J. J. Jackson. Durham: Duke University, 1973.

631. Henry, M. "Perceived Health Status of the Black Elderly in an Urban Area: Findings of a Survey Research Project." In *Health and the Black Aged: Proceedings of a Research Symposium*. ed. by W. Watson, J. Skinner, I. Lewis, S. Wesley, and B. Allen. Washington, D.C.: National Center on Black Aged, 1977.

632. Jackson, J. J. "Urban Black Americans." In *Ethnicity and Medical Care*, ed. by A. Harwood. Cambridge: Harvard University Press, 1981.

633. _____. "Special Health Problems of Aged Black." *Aging nos. 287-88* (1978): 15-20.

634. Johnson, E. F. "Look at it This Way: Some Aspects of the Drug Mix-up Problem Among Blacks, Poor, Aged and Female Patients." *Journal of the National Medical Association, 70*, no. 11 (1978): 745-47. See also: Women; Demographic and Socioeconomic Characteristics.

635. Kent, D. P. *Health Conditions, Social Adjustment, and Utilization of Community Resources Among Negro and White Aged.* Vol. 2. University Park: Pennsylvania State University, 1972. See also: Mental Health and Life Satisfaction; Support Services and Service Delivery.

636. Koch, H. K. "National Ambulatory Medical Care Survey." *Vital and Health Statistics,* Series 13, no. 33, Department of HEW. Hyattsville, Md: National Center for Health Statistics, 1978.

637. Koenig, R.; Goldner, N. S.; Kresojevich, R.; and Lockwood, G. "Ideas About Illness of Elderly Black and White in an Urban Hospital." *Aging and Human Development,* 2 (1971): 217-25.

638. Kovi, J. et al. "Gastric Cancer in American Negroes." *Cancer, 34,* no. 1 (1974): 765-70.

639. Kravits, J., and Schneider, J. "Health Care Need and Actual Use by Age, Race, and Income." In *Equity in Health Services: Empirical Analyses in Social Policy.* Cambridge: Ballinger, 1975. See also: Demographic and Socioeconomic Characteristics.

640. Lewis, E. A. "High Blood Pressure, Other Risk Factors and Longevity: the Insurance Viewpoint." *American Journal of Medicine, 55* (1973): 281-94. See also: Demographic and Socioeconomic Characteristics; Mortality.

641. Lewis, I. "The Study of Hypertension Compliance in a Group of Elderly Third World Patients." In *Health and the Black Aged,* ed. by W. Watson, J. Skinner, I. Lewis, S. Wesley, and B. Allen. Washington, D.C.: National Center on Black Aged, 1977.

642. McDowell, A. "Health Data on Aging Persons." In *Proceeding of the Research Conference on Minority Group Aged in the South,* ed. by J. J. Jackson. Durham: Duke University, 1972.

643. McPherson, J. R., et al. "Stature Change with Aging in Black Americans." *Journal of Gerontology, 33* (1978): 20-25.

644. Morgan, R. F. "The Adult Growth Examination: Preliminary Comparisons of Aging in Adults by Sex and Race." *Perceptual and Motor Skills, 27* (1968): 595-99.

645. Newman, G., et al. "Alterations in Neurologic Status with Age." *Journal of the American Geriatrics Society, 3,* no. 12 (1960): 915-17.

646. Nowlin, J. B. "Successful Aging: Health and Social Factors in an Interracial Population." *Black Aging, 2* (1977): 10-17. See also: Demographic and Socioeconomic Characteristics, Mental Health, and Life Satisfaction.

647. Paringer, L.; Bluck, J.; Feder, J.; and Holahan, J. *Health Status and Use of Medical Services: Evidence on the Poor, the Black, and the Rural Elderly.* Washington, D.C.: Urban Institute, 1979. See also: Rural; Demographic and Socioeconomic Characteristics.

648. Penn, J. J. "Nursing Care of the Aged." In *Proceedings of the Black Aged in the Future,* ed by J. J. Jackson. Durham: Duke University, 1973.

649. Peters, L. and Thomas, L. "A Community-based, Consumer Controlled Approach to Health Care for the Black Elderly." In *Health and the Black Aged: Proceedings of a Research Symposium,* ed. by W. Watson, J. Skinner, I. Lewis, S. Wesley, and B. Allen. Washington, D.C.: National Center on Black Aged, 1977.

650. Primm, B. "Poverty, Folk Remedies and Drug Misuse Among the Black Elderly." In *Health and the Black Aged: Proceedings of a Research Symposium,* ed. by W. Watson, J. Skinner, I. Lewis, S. Wesley, and B. Allen. Washington D.C.: National Center on Black Aged, 1977.

651. Roberts, J. "Blood Pressure Levels of Persons 65-74 Years, United States, 1971-1974." *Vital Health Statistics,* Series 11, no. 203, Department of HEW Publ. #78-1648. Washington, D.C.: U.S. Government Printing Office, 1977.

652. Shafer, S. Q. "Brain Infarction Risk Factors in Black New York City Stroke Patients." *Journal of Chronic Diseases, 27* (1974): 127-33.

653. Smith, L. "Hypertension and General Health in the Black Population." In *Minority Aging,* ed. by E. P. Stanford. San Diego: San Diego State University, 1975.

654. Staggers, F. "Carcinoma of the Prostate Gland in California: A Candid Look at Survival Trends in Regards to Stage, Race, and Social Class." In *Health and the Black Aged: Proceedings of a Research Symposium,* ed. by W. Watson, J. Skinner, I. Lewis, S. Wesley and B. Allen. Washington, D.C.: National Center on Black Aged, 1977. See also: Demographic and Socioeconomic Characteristics; Mortality.

655. Szczeklik, A.; Dischinger, P.; Kueppers, F.; Tyroler, H. A.; Hames, C.; Cassell, J. C.; and Creagan, S. "Blood Fibrinolytic Activity, Social Class and Habitual Physical Activity — II. A Study of Black and White Men in Southern Georgia." *Journal of Chronic Diseases, 33* (1980): 291-99. See also: Demographic and Socioeconomic Characteristics.

656. Thompson, L. W., et al. "Relation of Serum Cholesterol to Age, Sex, and Race in an Elderly Community Group." *Journal of Gerontology, 20* (1965): 160-64.

657. Thornhill, H.; Todd, C.; and Anderson, A. "Mobility Among the Physically Impaired Black Aged." In *Health and the Black Aged: Proceedings of a Research Symposium*, ed. by W. Watson, J. Skinner, I. Lewis, S. Wesley, and B. Allen. Washington, D.C.: National Center on Black Aged, 1977.

658. U.S. Department of HEW, Public Health Service, *Blood Pressure of Adults by Race and Area, 1960-62*. PHS no. 1000, Series 100, no. 5, Washington, D.C.: 1964.

659. Watson, W.; Skinner, J.; Lewis, I.; Wesley, J.; Allen, B., eds. *Health and the Black Aged: Proceedings of a Research Symposium*. Washington, D.C.: National Center on Black Aged, 1977.

660. Weaver, J. L. "Personal Health Care: A Major Concern for Minority Aged." In *Comprehensive Service Delivery System for the Minority Aged*, ed. by E. P. Stanford. San Diego: San Diego State University, 1977.

661. Whanger, A., and Wang, H. S. "Clinical Correlates of the Vibratory Sense in Elderly Psychiatric Patients." *Journal of Gerontology*, 29, no. 1 (1974): 39-45.

662. Wright, R.; Berg, W. E.; and Creecy, R. "Medical Care and the Elderly: An Exploratory Analysis of Factors Involved in the Use of Physicians' Services by Black and White Elderly." *Journal of Minority Aging*, 5, no. 1 (1979): 123-29. See also: Support Services and Service Delivery.

663. Young, J. L., et al. "Incidence of Cancer in the United States Blacks." *Cancer Research*, 35 (1975): 3523-36.
See also 141, 153, 160.

Housing

664. Isserman, A. J. "Housing for the Aged Blacks." In *Proceedings of the Black Aged in the Future*, ed. by J. J. Jackson. Durham: Duke University, 1973.

665. Jackson, H. D. "Housing and Geriatric Centers for Aging and Aged Blacks." In *Proceedings of the Black Aged in the Future*, ed. by J. J. Jackson. Durham: Duke University, 1973. See also: Nursing Homes and Institutionalization; Support Services and Service Delivery.

666. Jackson, J. J. "Social Impacts of Housing Relocation upon Urban Low-Income Black Aged." *Gerontologist*, 12 (1972): 32-37. See also: Demographic and Socioeconomic Characteristics.

667. Johnson, R. "Barriers to Adequate Housing for Elderly Blacks." *Aging Nos. 287-88* (1978): 33-39. See also: Prejudice, Discrimination, Racism, and Stereotyping.

668.   National Center on Black Aged. "Deplorable Conditions of Housing for Aged Blacks." *NCBA Technical Bulletin Series*, August 1975.

669.   Quadagno, J. S., et al. "Maintaining Social Distance in a Racially Integrated Retirement Community." *Black Aging*, 3, nos. 4 & 5 (1978): 97-112. See also: Work and Retirement; Prejudice, Discrimination, Racism, and Stereotyping.

670.   Wilson, J. L. "Geriatric Experiences with the Negro Aged." *Geriatrics*, 8 (1953): 88-92.

See also 177.

Leisure

671.   Lambing, M. L. B. "Leisure Time Pursuits Among Retired Blacks by Social Status." *Gerontologist*, 12 (1972): 363-67. See also: Work and Retirement; Demographic and Socioeconomic Characteristics.

Marriage and Family

672.   Angel, R., and Tienda, M. "Determinants of Extended Household Structure: Cultural Pattern or Economic Need?" *American Journal of Sociology*, 87 (May 1982): 1360-83.

673.   Aschenbrenner, J. "Extended Families Among Black Americans." *Journal of Comparative Family Studies*, 4 (1973): 257-68.

674.   Bernard, J. *Marriage and Family Among Negroes*. Englewood Cliffs: Prentice-Hall, 1966.

675.   Bianchi, S., and Farley, R. "Racial Differences in Family Living Arrangements and Economic Well-Being: An Analysis of Recent Trends." *Journal of Marriage and the Family*, 41 (1979): 537-51.

676.   Billingsley, A. *Black Families in White America*. Englewood Cliffs: Prentice-Hall, 1968.

677.   Birmingham, S. *Certain People: America's Black Elite*. Boston: Little, Brown, & Co., 1977. See also: Demographic and Socioeconomic Characteristics.

678.   Brunswick, A. F. "What Generation Gap? A Comparison of Some Differences Among Blacks and Whites." *Social Problems*, 17 (1969-1970): 358-70.

679.   Cantor, M.; Rosenthal, K.; and Wilker, L. "Social and Family Relationships of Black Aged Women in New York City." *Journal of Minority Aging*, 4 (1979): 50-61. See also: Social Participation and Friendships; Women.

680. Cazenave, N. "Family Violence and Aging Blacks: Theoretical Perspectives and Research Possibilities." *Journal of Minority Aging, 4* (1979): 99-108.

681. Frazier, E. F. *The Negro Family in Chicago.* Chicago: University of Chicago Press, 1932. See also Rural.

682. _____. *The Negro Family in the United States.* Chicago: University of Chicago Press, 1966.

683. Gillespie, B. J. "The Black Family in the American Ecomony." *Journal of Afro-American Issues, 3* (Summer-Fall 1975): 324-35. See also: Demographic and Socioeconomic Characteristics.

684. _____. "Black Grandparents: Childhood Socialization." *Journal of Afro-American Issues, 4,* nos. 3 & 4 (1976): 432-41.

685. Harrison-Ross, P. *The Black Child: A Parents' Guide.* New York: Wyden, 1973.

686. Hays, W. C., and Mindel, C. H. "Extended Kinship Relations in Black and White Families." *Journal of Marriage and the Family, 35,* no. 1 (1973): 51-57.

687. Hill, R. B. *The Strengths of Black Families.* New York: Emerson Hall, 1971.

688. Huling, W. E. "Evolving Family Roles for the Black Elderly." *Aging* (September/October 1978): 21-27.

689. Jackson, J. J. "Aging Black Families and Federal Policies: Some Critical Issues." *Journal of Minority Aging, 4* (1979): 76-87. See also: Social Policy and Politics.

690. _____. "Family Organization and Ideology." In *Comparative Studies of Negroes and Whites in the United States,* ed. by R. M. Dreger and K. S. Miller. New York: Seminar Press, 1973.

691. _____. "Kinship Relations Among Urban Blacks." *Journal of Social and Behavioral Sciences, 16* (1970): 5-17.

692. _____. "Marital Life Among Aging Blacks." *Family Coordinator, 21* (1972): 21-27.

693. _____. "Negro Aged Parents and Adult Children: Their Affective Relationships." *Varia, 2* (1969): 1-14.

694. _____. "Sex and Social Class Variations in Black Aged Parent-Adult Child Relationships." *Aging and Human Development, 2* (1971): 96-107. See also: Demographic and Socioeconomic Characteristics.

695. Jones, F. C. "The Lofty Role of the Black Grandmother." *Crisis, 80* (1973): 19-21. See also: Women.

696. Langston, E. J. "Kith & Kin; Natural Support Systems: Their Implications for Policies and Programs for the Black Aged." In *Minority Aging: Policy Issues for the 80's*, ed. by E. P. Stanford. San Diego: San Diego State University, 1980. See also: Support Services and Service Delivery; Social Policy and Politics.

697. Lopata, H. Z. *Social and Family Relations of Black and White Widows in Urban Communities.* Washington, D.C.: Administration on Aging Publication, no. 25, HEW, 1970. See also: Women.

698. Martin, E. P. and Martin, J. M. *The Black Extended Family.* Chicago: University of Chicago Press, 1978.

699. Scanzoni, J. H. *The Black Family in Modern Society.* Boston: Allyn and Bacon, 1971.

700. Smith, D. S.; Dahlin, M.; and Friedberger, M. "The Family Structure of the Older Black Population in the American South in 1880 and 1900." *Sociology and Social Research, 63,* no. 3 (1979): 544-65.

701. Stack, C. B. *All Our Kin: Strategies for Survival in a Black Community.* New York: Harper and Row, 1974.

702. Staples, R. "The Black American Family." In *Ethnic Families in America*, 2d ed., ed. by C. H. Mindel and R. W. Habenstein. New York: Elsevier, 1981.

703. Yelder, J. "The Influence of Culture on Family Relations: The Black American Experience." *Aging Parents.* Los Angeles: University of Southern California, 1979.

See also 194.

Mental Health and Life Satisfaction

704. Beard, V. H. "Health Status of a Successful Black Aged Population Related to Life Satisfaction and Self-Concept." In *Health and the Black Aged: Proceedings of a Research Symposium*, ed. by W. Watson, J. Skinner, I. Lewis, S. Wesley, and B. Allen. Washington, D.C.: National Center on Black Aged, 1977. See also: Health, Medicine, and Folk Medicine.

705. Butler, R. N. "Excerpts on Black Aged from the Urban League News: Social Factors Affect Mental Health of Aged." In *Growing Old in America*, ed. by B. B. Hess. New Brunswick: Transaction, 1976.

706. Carter, J. H. "A Psychiatric Strategy for Aged Blacks in the Future." In *Proceedings of the Black Aged in the Future*, ed. by J. J. Jackson. Durham: Duke University, 1973.

707. _____. "Recognizing Psychiatric Symptoms in Black America." *Geriatrics*, 29 (1974): 95-99.

708. _____. "The Black Aged: A Strategy for Future Mental Health Services." *Journal of the American Geriatrics Society*, 26, no. 12 (1978): 553-56.

709. Clemente, F. and Sauer, W. J. "Race and Morale of the Urban Aged." *Gerontologist*, 14 (1974): 342-44. See also: Rural.

710. Creecy, R.; Wright, R.; and Berg, W. E. "Correlates of Loneliness Among the Black Elderly." *Journal of Activities, Adaptation and Aging*, 3, no. 2 (Winter 1983): 9-16.

711. _____. "Morale and Informal Activity with Friends Among Black and White Elderly." *Gerontologist*, 19 (1979): 544-47.

712. Elam, L. C. "Critical Factors for Mental Health in Aging Black Populations." In *Ethnicity, Mental Health, and Aging: Proceedings of a Two-day Workshop*. Los Angeles: The Ethel Percy Andrus Gerontology Center, University of Southern California, 1970.

713. Faulkner, A.; Heisel, M.; and Simms, P. "Life Strengths and Life Stresses: Explorations in the Measurement of Mental Health of the Black Aged." *American Journal of Orthopsychiatry*, 45 (1975): 102-10.

714. Furgess, A. "Reflections on Counseling Elderly Blacks." *Journal of Non-White Concerns in Personnel Guidance*, 5, no. 10 (1976): 45-48.

715. Gary, L., ed. *Mental Health, A Challenge to the Black Community*. Philadelphia: Dorrance, 1980.

716. _____ "Mental Health: The Problem and the Product." In *Mental Health: A Challenge to the Black Community*, ed. by L. Gary. Philadelphia: Dorrance, 1980.

717. Gatz, M.; Gease, E.; Tyler, F.; and Moran, J. "Psychosocial Competence Characteristics of Black and White Women: The Constraining Effects of Triple Jeopardy." *The Black Scholar: Journal of Black Studies*, 13, no. 1 (1982): 5-12. See also: Women.

718. Gibson, R. C. "Blacks at Midlife: Personal Resources and Coping." In *Annals of the American Academy of Political and Social Science*, 464 (Nov. 1982): 79-90.

719.   Gilson, P., and Coats, S. "A Study of Morale in Low Income Blacks."
        Journal of Gerontological Nursing, 6, no. 7 (1980): 385-88. See also:
        Demographic and Socioeconomic Characteristics.

720.   Golden, H. M. "Life Satisfaction Among Black Elderly in the Inner
        City." *Black Aging*, 2, nos. 2 & 3 (1976-1977): 21-43.

721.   Hawkins, B. "Mental Health and the Black Aged." In *Mental Health:
        A Challenge to the Black Community*, ed. by L. Gary. Philadelphia:
        Dorrance, 1978.

722.   Hawley, I. B. "Psychological Aspects of Aging." In *Proceedings of the
        Workshop Series on the Black Aged and Aging and the Conference on the
        Black Aged and Aging*, ed. by J. Dorsett-Robinson. Carbondale:
        Southern Illinois University, 1974.

723.   Himes, J., and Hamlett, M. "The Assessment of Adjustment of
        Aged Negro Women in a Southern City." *Phylon*, 23 (Summer 1962):
        139-47. See also: Women.

724.   Holley, M. R. "Components of Life Satisfaction of Older Texans: A
        Multi-Dimensional Model." *Black Aging*, 3 (1978): 113-21.

725.   Jackson, J. J. "Epidemiological Aspects of Mental Illness Among
        Aged Black Women and Men." *Journal of Minority Aging*, 4 (1979):
        76-87. See also: Women.

726.   Jackson, J.; Bacon, J.; and Peterson, J. "Correlates of Adjustment in
        Urban Black Aged." *Gerontologist*, 14, no. 5, pt. 2 (1974): 74.

727.   _____. "Life Satisfaction Among Black Urban Elderly." *Interna-
        tional Journal of Aging and Human Development*, 8, no. 2 (1977-1978):
        169-79.

728.   Jackson, J. S.; Chatters, L. M.; and Neighbors, H. W. "The Mental
        Health Status of Older Black Americans: A National Study." *The
        Black Scholar: Journal of Black Studies*, 13, no. 1 (1982): 21-35.

729.   Lindsay, I. B. "Coping Capacities of the Black Aged." In *No Longer
        Young: The Older Woman in America—Occasional Papers in Gerontol-
        ogy*, no. 11. Ann Arbor: Institute of Gerontology, University of
        Michigan-Wayne State University, 1975. See also: Women.

730.   Penn, N. E. "Ethnicity and Aging in Elderly Black Women: Some
        Mental Health Characteristics." In *Health and the Black Aged: Pro-
        ceedings of a Research Symposium*, ed. by W. Watson, J. Skinner,
        I. Lewis, S. Wesley and B. Allen Washington, D.C.: National Center
        on Black Aged, 1977. See also: Women.

731.   Peterson, J., and Thomas, L. "The Social Psychology of Black Aging: The Effects of Self-Esteem and Perceived Control on the Adjustment of Older Black Adults." In *Health and the Black Aged: Proceedings of a Research Symposium*, ed. by W. Watson, J. Skinner, I. Lewis, S. Wesley, and B. Allen. Washington, D.C.: National Center on Black Aged, 1977.

732.   Rao, V. N., and Rao, V. V. P. "Life Satisfaction in the Black Elderly: An Exploratory Study." *International Journal of Aging and Human Development, 14*, no. 1 (1981-82): 55-65.

733.   Sager, C. J.; Brayboy, T. L.; and Waxenberg, B. R. *Black Ghetto Family in Therapy: A Laboratory Experience.* New York: Grove, 1970.

734.   Sauer, W. "Morale of the Urban Aged: A Regression Analysis by Race." *Journal of Gerontology, 32*, no. 5 (1977): 600-08.

735.   Shader, R., and Tracy, M. "On Being Black, Old and Emotionally Troubled: How Little is Known." *Psychiatric Opinion, 10* (1973): 26-32.

736.   Smith, A. D. "Life Satisfaction and Activity Preferences of Black Female Participants in Senior Citizens' Centers: An Investigative Inquiry." *Black Aging, 3*, nos. 1 & 2 (1977): 8-13. See also: Women.

737.   Solomon, B. "Ethnicity, Mental Health and the Older Black Aged." In *Ethnicity, Mental Health and Aging.* Los Angeles: The Ethel Percy Andrus Gerontology Center, University of Southern California, 1970. See also: Prejudice, Discrimination, Racism, and Stereotyping.

738.   Stanford, E. P. "Mental Health Perspectives on Black Aging." In *Health Care and the Black Aged: A Call for Radical Change*, ed. by D. J. Davis, M. Johnson, G. Harris, and D. Wong. Washington, D.C.: National Center on Black Aged, 1977.

739.   Stretch, J. J. "Are Aged Blacks Who Manifest Differences in Community Security also Different in Coping Reaction?" *International Journal of Aging and Human Development, 7* (1976): 171-84.

740.   Swanson, W. C., and Harter, C. L. "How Do Elderly Blacks Cope in New Orleans?" *Aging and Human Development, 2* (1971): 210-16. See also: Death and Dying.

741.   Taylor, S. P. "Mental Health and Successful Coping Among Aged Black Women." In *Minority Aging: Sociological and Social Psychological Issues*, ed. by R. C. Manuel. Westport, Conn.: Greenwood Press, 1982. See also: Women.

742.   Thornton, C. I., and Carter, J. H. "Improving Mental Health Ser-
       vices to Low Income Blacks." *Journal of the American Medical Associa-
       tion*, 67, no. 2 (1975): 167-70. See also: Support Services and Service
       Delivery; Demographic and Socioeconomic Characteristics.

743.   Thurmond, G. T., and Belcher, J. C. "Dimensions of Disengagement
       Among Black and White Rural Elderly." *International Journal of Aging
       and Human Development*, 12, no. 4 (1980-81): 245-66. See also: Rural.

744.   Usui, W. M.; Keil, T. J.; and Phillips, D. C. "Determinants of Life
       Satisfaction: A Note on a Race-Interaction Hypothesis." *Journal of
       Gerontology*, 38, no. 1 (1983): 107-10.

745.   Ward, R. A., and Kilburn, H. "Community Access and Satisfaction:
       Racial Differences in Later Life." *International Journal of Aging and
       Human Development*, 16, no. 3 (1983): 209-19.

746.   Watson, W. *Stress and Old Age: A Case Study of Black Aging and
       Transplantation Shock*. New Brunswick, N. J.: Transaction Books,
       1980.

See also 219, 227.

Mortality

747.   Crimmins, E. "The Changing Pattern of American Mortality
       Decline, 1940-77, and Its Implications for the Future." *Population and
       Development Review*, 7 (1981): 229-53. See also: Health, Medicine,
       and Folk Medicine.

748.   Demeny, P., and Gingrich, P. "A Reconsideration of Negro-White
       Mortality Differentials in the United States." *Demography*, 4 (1967):
       820-37. See also: Health, Medicine, and Folk Medicine.

749.   Gorwitz, K. "On the Decrease in Black Male Life Expectancy." In
       *1974 Proceedings of the Social Statistics Section of the American Statistical
       Association*. Washington, D.C.: American Statistical Association,
       1975. See also: Health, Medicine, and Folk Medicine.

750.   Gorwitz, K., and Dennis, R. "On the Decrease in Life Expectancy of
       Black Males in Michigan." *Public Health Reports*, 91 (1976): 141-45.
       See also: Health, Medicine, and Folk Medicine.

751.   Jackson, J. J. "Death Rates of Aged Blacks and Whites, United
       States, 1964-1978." *The Black Scholar: Journal of Black Studies*, 13, no.
       1 (1982): 36-48. See also: Health, Medicine, and Folk Medicine.

752.   Manton, K. "Sex and Race Specific Mortality Differentials in Multi-
       ple Cause of Death Date." *Gerontologist*, 20, no. 4 (1980): 481-93.

753. _____. "Temporal and Age Variation of United States Black/White Cause-Specific Mortality Differentials: A Study of the Recent Changes in the Relative Health Status of the United States Black Population." *Gerontologist*, 22, no. 2 (1982): 170-79.

754. Manton, K., and Poss, S. S. "The Black/White Mortality Crossover: Investigation from the Perspective of the Components of Aging." *Gerontologist*, 19 (1979): 291-300. See also: Health, Medicine, and Folk Medicine.

755. _____. "The Black/White Mortality Crossover: Possible Racial Differences in the Intrinsic Rate of Aging." *Black Aging*, 3 (1978): 43-52. See also: Health, Medicine and Folk Medicine.

756. Manton, K., and Stallard, E. "Methods of Evaluating the Heterogeneity of Aging Processes in Human Populations Using Vital Statistics Data: Explaining the Black/White Mortality Crossover by a Model of Mortality Selection." *Human Biology*, 53 (1981): 47-67. See also: Health, Medicine, and Folk Medicine.

757. Rives, Jr., N. W. "The Effect of Census Errors on Life Table Estimates of Black Mortality." *Public Health Briefs*, 67 (1977): 867-68.

758. Shafer, S. Q., et al. "The Contribution of Nonaneurysmal Intracranial Hemorrhage to Stroke Mortality in New York City Blacks." *Strokes*, 4 (1973): 928-32. See also: Health, Medicine, and Folk Medicine.

759. Sutton, G. F. "Assessing Mortality and Morbidity Disadvantages of the Black Population of the United States." *Social Biology*, 18, no. 4 (1971): 369-83.

760. Thornton, R. J., and Nam, C. B. "The Lower Mortality Rates of Nonwhites at Older Ages: An Enigma in Demographic Analyses." *Research Reports in Social Science*, 2, no. 1 (1968). See also: Health, Medicine, and Folk Medicine.

761. Zelnik, M. "Age Patterns of Mortality of American Negros, 1900-02 to 1959-61." *Journal of American Statistical Association*, 64 (1969): 433-51. See also: Health, Medicine, and Folk Medicine.
See also 243, 247, 252.

Nursing Homes and Institutionalization

762. Gibbs, E. "Nursing Home Action." In *Action for Aged Blacks: When? A Conference of the National Caucus on the Black Aged*, ed. by J. J. Jackson. Washington, D.C.: National Caucus on Black Aged, 1973.

763. Jackson, J. J. "Help Me Somebody, I'se an Old Black Standing in the Need of Institutionalizing." *Psychiatric Opinion, 10* (1973): 6-16.

764. Jackson, J. J. "Really, There Are Existing Alternatives to Institutionalization Care for Aged Blacks." In *National Conference on Alternatives to Institutional Care for Older Americans: Practice and Planning,* ed. by Eric Pfeiffer. Durham: Duke University, 1973.

765. Kart, C. S., and Beckham, B. L. "Black-White Differentials in the Institutionalization of the Elderly: A Temporal Analysis." *Social Forces, 54,* no. 4 (June 1976): 901-10.

766. Manard, B. B., et al. *Old-Age Institutions.* Lexington, Mass: Lexington Books, 1975.

767. National Council on Aging. *The Golden Years – A Tarnished Myth.* New York: National Council on Aging, 1970.

768. Pollard, L. J. "Black Beneficial Societies and the Home for Aged and Infirm Colored Persons: A Research Note." *Phylon, 41,* no. 3 (1980): 230-34.

769. Rebeck, A. H. *A Study of the Development in Programs for the Care of the Aged: With Emphasis on New York State and New York City.* New York: New York State Department of Social Welfare, May 1, 1943.

770. U.S. Dept. of Labor. "Home For Aged Colored Persons." *Monthly Labor Review, 29* (August 1929): 284-88.

771. Weinstock, C. and Bennett, R. "Problems in Communication to Nurses Among Residents of a Racially Heterogeneous Nursing Home." *Gerontologist, 8* (1968): 72-75.

772. Wershow, H. J. "Inadequate Census Data on Black Nursing Home Patients." *Gerontologist, 16* (1976): 86-87.

See also 255.

Prejudice, Discrimination, Racism, and Stereotyping

773. Carter, J. H. "Differential Treatment of the Elderly Black: Victims of Stereotyping." *Postgraduate Medicine, 52* (1972): 211-14.

774. _____. "Excerpts on Black Aged from the Urban League News: Racism in the Psychiatric Care of Older Blacks." In *Growing Old in America,* ed. by B. B. Hess. New Brunswick: Transaction, 1976. See also: Mental Health and Life Satisfaction.

775. _____. "Psychiatry's Insensitivity to Racism and Aging." *Psychiatric Opinion, 10,* no. 6 (1973): 21-25. See also: Mental Health and Life Satisfaction.

776. Cooper, R.; Steinhauer, M.; Miller, W.; David, R.; and Schatzkin, A. "Racism, Society, and Disease: An Exploration of the Social and Biological Mechanisms of Differential Mortality." *International Journal of Health Services, 11* (1981): 389-413. See also: Health, Medicine, and Folk Medicine; Mortality.

777. Golden, H. M. "The Myth of Homogeneity Among Black Elderly." *Black Aging, 1, 2, 3* (1975-1976): 1-11.

778. Jackson, J. J. "Aged Blacks: A Potpourri Towards the Reduction of Racial Inequities." *Phylon, 32* (1971): 260-80. See also: General.

779. Lewis, H. *Blackways of Kent.* Chapel Hill: University of North Carolina Press, 1950.

780. McClory, R. "Triple Jeopardy: Old, Black and Poor." *Race Relations Reporter, 5* (September 1974).

781. National Urban League. *Double Jeopardy: The Older Negro in America Today.* New York: National Urban League, 1964.

782. Thune, J. M. "Racial Attitudes of Olders Adults." *Gerontologist, 7* (1967): 179-82.

783. U.S. Congress, Senate, Special Committee on Aging. "The Multiple Hazards of Age and Race: The Situation of Aged Blacks in the United States: A Working Paper." Washington, D.C.: U.S. Government Printing Office, 1971.

See also 279.

Religion

784. Carter, A. C. "Religion and the Black Elderly: The Historical Basis of Social and Psychological Concerns." In *Minority Aging: Sociological and Social Psychological Issues*, ed. by R. C. Manuel. Westport, Conn.: Greenwood Press, 1982.

785. Heisel, M. A., and Faulkner, A. O. "Religiosity in an Older Black Population." *Gerontologist, 22*, no. 4 (1982): 354-58.

786. Jericho, B. J. "Longitudinal Changes in Religious Activity Subscores of Aged Blacks." *Black Aging, 2* (1977): 17-24.

787. Walker, B. J. "How Organized Religion Can and Should Meet the Needs of Aged Blacks." In *Action for Aged Blacks: A Conference of the National Caucus on the Black Aged*, ed. by J. J. Jackson. Washington, D.C.: National Caucus on the Black Aged, 1973. See also: Support Services and Service Delivery.

788.   Walls, W. J. *The African Methodist Episcopal Zion Church: Reality of the Black Church*. Charlotte, N. C.: A.M.E. Zion, 1974.

Rural

789.   Auerbach, A. "Some Observations on the Black Aged in the Rural Midwest." *Journal of Social Welfare* (Winter 1975-76): 53-61.

790.   Coppin, V. "Black Folks, Rural Style '77." In *Retirement: Concepts and Realities*, ed. by E. P. Stanford. San Diego: San Diego State University, 1978. See also: Work and Retirement.

791.   Holmes, J. S. "Urban and Rural Comparisons." In *Proceedings of the Workshop Series on the Black Aged and Aging and the Conference on the Black Aged and Aging*, ed. by J. Dorsett-Robinson. Carbondale: Southern Illinois University, 1974.

792.   Jackson, J. J. "Aged Negroes and Their Cultural Departures from Stereotypes and Rural-Urban Differences." *Gerontologist*, 10 (1970): 140-45. See also: General.

793.   Jackson, J. J., and Davis, A. "Characteristic Patterns of Aged, Rural Negroes in Macon County." In *A Survey of Selected Socioeconomic Characteristics of Macon County*, ed. by B. C. Johnson. Tuskegee: Macon County Community Action Office, 1966. See also: Demographic and Socioeconomic Characteristics.

794.   Jackson, J. J., and Ball, M. "A Comparison of Rural and Urban Georgia Aged Negroes." *Journal of the Association of Social Science Teachers*, 12 (1966): 32-37.

795.   Kivett, V. R. "The Importance of Race to the Life Situation of the Rural Elderly." *The Black Scholar: Journal of Black Studies*, 13, no. 1 (1982): 13-20.

796.   Rosen, C. E. "A Comparison of Black and White Rural Elderly." *Black Aging*, 3, no. 3 (1978): 60-65.

797.   Smith, S. H. "The Older Rural Negro." In *Older Rural Americans*, ed. by G. Youmans. Lexington: University of Kentucky Press, 1967.

Slavery

798.   Armstrong, O. K. *Old Massa's People: The Old Slaves Tell Their Story*. Indianapolis: Bobbs-Merrill Co., 1931.

799.   Ball, C. *Slavery in the United States: A Narrative of the Life and Adventures of Charles Ball, A Black Man, Who Lived Forty Years in Maryland, South Carolina and Georgia, as a Slave Under Various Masters, and was One Year in the Navy with Commodore Barney During the Late War*. Lewiston, Pa.: J. W. Shugert, 1836.

800. Herskovits, M. J. *The Myths of the Negro Past.* New York: Harper and Brothers, 1941.

801. Jacobs, H. "The Good Grandmother." In *The Freedman's Book*, ed. by Maria Child. Boston: Ticknor and Fields, 1865. See also: Women.

802. Steward, A. *Twenty-two Years a Slave, and Forty Years a Freeman.* Rochester, New York: William Alling, Publisher, 1857.

803. Syrgley, F. D. *Seventy Years In Dixie.* Nashille: Gospel Advocate, 1891.

Social Participation and Friendships

804. Feagin, J. "A Note on the Friendship Ties of Black Urbanites." *Social Forces*, 49 (1970-71): 303-8.

805. Hoyt, D., and Babchuk, N. "Ethnicity and the Voluntary Associations of the Aged." *Ethnicity*, 8 (1981): 67-81.

806. Jackson, J. J. "Comparative Lifestyles and Family and Friends Relationships Among Older Black Women." *Family Coordinator, 21* (1972): 477-85. See also: Women; Marriage and Family.

807. Kivett, V. R. "Loneliness and the Rural Black Elderly: Perspectives on Intervention." *Black Aging, 3* (1978): 160-66. See also: Support Services and Service Delivery; Rural.

808. Klobus-Edwards, P.; Edwards, J.; and Klemmack, D. "Differences in Social Participation: Blacks and Whites." *Social Forces, 56* (1978): 1035-52.

809. Lopata, H. Z. "Social Relations of Black and White Widowed Women in a Northern Metropolis." *American Journal of Sociology, 78* (1973): 1003-10. See also: Women; Marriage and Family.

810. Rubenstein, D. "An Examination of Social Participation Found Among a National Sample of Black and White Elderly." *Aging and Human Development, 2* (1971): 172-88.

811. Wellin, E., and Boyer, E. "Adjustments of Black and White Elderly to the Same Adaptive Niche." *Anthropological Quarterly, 52* (1979): 39-48.

See also 295.

Social Policy and Politics

812. Cairo, C. "Why the National Caucus on the Black Aged?" *Harvest Years, 11* (1971): 13-18.

813. Chunn, J. "The Black Aged and Social Policy." *Aging* (September-October 1978): 10-14.

814. Craig, D. "Aged Blacks: The Story of Cleveland, Ohio." In *Action for Aged Blacks: When? A Conference on the National Caucus on the Black Aged*, ed. by J. J. Jackson. Washington, D.C.: National Caucus on the Black Aged, 1973.

815. Flemming, A. C. "Action and Aged Blacks: The Post-White House Conference on Aging." In *Action for Aged Blacks: When? A Conference of the National Caucus on the Black Aged*, ed. by J. J. Jackson. Washington, D.C.: National Caucus on the Black Aged, 1973.

816. Jackson, H. C. "Black Advocacy, Techniques and Trials." In *Advocacy and Age: Issues, Experiences, Strategies*, ed. by P. A. Kerschner. Los Angeles: University of Southern California Press, 1976.

817. _____. "National Caucus on the Black Aged: A Progress Report." *Aging and Human Development*, 2 (1971): 226-31.

818. _____. "Social Policy Which Facilitates These Services." In *Community Services and the Black Elderly*, ed. by R. H. Davis. Los Angeles: The Ethel Percy Andrus Gerontology Center, University of Southern California, 1972. See also: Support Services and Service Delivery.

819. _____. "The White House Conference on Aging and Black Aged." In *Proceedings of the Research Conference on the Minority Group Aged in the South*, ed. by J. J. Jackson. Durham: Duke University, 1972. See also: Support Services and Service Delivery.

820. Jackson, J. J. "Action and Non-Action." In *Action for Aged Blacks: When? Proceedings of the Annual Conference of the National Caucus on the Black Aged*. Washington, D.C., May 16-17, 1973.

821. _____. "Aged Blacks: A Potpourri in the Direction of the Reduction of Inequities." *Phylon*, 32, no. 3 (1971): 260-80.

822. _____. "NCBA, Black Aged and Politics." *The Annals of the American Academy of Political and Social Science*, 415 (1974): 138-59.

823. _____, ed. *Action for Aged Blacks: When? A Conference of the National Caucus on the Black Aged*. Washington, D.C.: National Caucus on the Aged, 1973.

824. Jackson, M. "The Black Aged: Review and Analysis." In *Understanding Minority Aging: Perspectives and Sources*, ed. by J. B. Cuellar, E. P. Stanford, and D. I. Miller-Soule. San Diego: San Diego State University, 1982.

825.   Kastenbaum, R. J. "National Caucus on the Black Aged." *Aging and Human Development*, 2 (1971): 1-2.

826.   Lindsay, I. B. "The Multiple Hazards of Age and Race. The Situation of Aged Blacks in the United States." Report #92-450. Washington, D.C.: U.S. Government Printing Office, 1971. See also: Demographic and Socioeconomic Characteristics.

827.   Mitchell, P. J. "Mutual National Caucus on the Black Aged (NCBA) and the Congressional Black Caucus (CBC) Concerns about Aged Blacks and Recommended Legislation for Action." In *Action for Aged Blacks: When? A Conference of the National Caucus on the Black Aged*, ed. by J. J. Jackson. Washington, D.C.: National Caucus on the Black Aged, 1973.

828.   Robinson, H. "Political Action and the Black Aged." In *Action for Aged Blacks: When? A Conference of the National Caucus on the Black Aged*, ed. by J. J. Jackson. Washington, D.C.: National Caucus on the Black Aged, 1973.

829.   Sheppard, N. A. "A Federal Perspective on the Black Aged: From Concern to Action." *Aging*, Nos. 287-88 (1978): 28-32.

830.   U.S. Congress, Senate, Special Committee on Aging. *A Pre-White House Conference on Aging. Summary of Development and Data*. 92nd Congress, 1st Session, 1971, Rpt. no. 92-505.

831.   White House Conference on Aging. "The Aging and Aged Blacks." *Toward a National Policy on Aging*, 2. Washington, D.C.: U.S. Government Printing Office, 1971.

832.   _____. *Reports of the Special Concerns Sessions (1971): The Aging and the Aged Blacks*. Washington, D.C.: U.S. Government Printing Office, 1971.

Social Security and Old Age Assistance

833.   Davis, F. G. "The Impact of Social Security Taxes upon the Poor: The Case of the Black Community." In *Economics of Aging*. Ann Arbor: Institute of Gerontology, University of Michigan-Wayne State University, 1976. See also: Social Policy and Politics.

834.   _____. *The Black Community's Social Security*. Washington, D.C.: University Press of America, 1978.

835.   Henderson, G. "The Negro Recipient of Old-Age Assistance: Results of Discrimination." *Social Casework*, 46 (1965): 208-14. See also: Prejudice, Discrimination, Racism, and Stereotyping.

836.   Thompson, G. B. "Black Social Security Benefits: Trends 1960-1973."
       Social Security Bulletin, 38 (April 1975): 30-40.

Support Services and Service Delivery

837.   Andersen, R.; Andersen, O. W.; and Kravits, J. *Equity in Health Services: Empirical Analyses in Social Policy.* Cambridge: Ballinger Publishing Co., 1975. See also: Health, Medicine, and Folk Medicine; Social Policy and Politics.

838.   Anderson, P. "Support Services and Aged Blacks." *Black Aging, 3,* no. 3 (1978): 53-59.

839.   Beattie, Jr., W. M. "The Aging Negro: Some Implications for Social Welfare Services." *Phylon, 21* (1960): 131-35.

840.   Clemente, F.; Rexroad, P. A.; and Hirsch, C. "The Participation of Black Aged in Voluntary Associations." *Journal of Gerontology, 30* (1975): 469-78. See also: Social Participation and Friendships.

841.   Davis, R. H., ed. *Community Services and the Black Elderly.* Los Angeles: The Ethel Percy Andrus Gerontology Center, University of Southern California, 1972.

842.   _____. ed. *Workshop on Community Services and the Black Elderly.* Los Angeles: The Ethel Percy Andrus Gerontology Center, University of Southern California, 1972.

843.   Downing, R. A., and Copeland, E. J. "Services for the Black Elderly: National or Local Problems?" *Journal of Gerontological Social Work, 2,* no. 4 (1980): 289-303. See also: Social Policy and Politics.

844.   Engler, M., and Mayer, M. *Home-Delivered Meals Survey Third Report: Description of and Comparisons Between Black and White Elderly Receiving Home-Delivered Meals with Respect to Functional Ability, Sources of Support and Demographics.* New York: Bureau of Research, Planning and Policy Analysis, New York City Dept. for the Aging, February 1982. See also: Food and Nutrition.

845.   Faulkner, A. O. "The Black Aged as Good Neighbors: An Experiment in Volunteer Service." *Gerontologist, 15* (1975): 554-59. See also: Social Participation and Friendships.

846.   Hall, G., and Mathiasen, G., eds. *Guide to Development of Protective Services for Older People.* Springfield, Ill.: Charles C. Thomas, 1973. See also: Social Policy and Politics.

847.   Hudson, G. H. "Some Special Problems of Older Black Americans." *The Crisis, 83,* no. 3 (1976): 88-90.

848. Jackson, H. C. "Easing the Plight of the Black Elderly." *Perspectives on Aging*, 4 (1975): 21-22.

849. Kent, D. P., and Hirsch, C. *Needs and Use of Services Among Negro and White Aged*. Vol. 1. "Social and Economic Conditions of Negro and White Aged Residents of Urban Neighborhoods of Low Socio-Economic Status." University Park: Pennsylvania State University, 1971.

850. Leyhe, D; Gartside, F; and Proctor, D. "Medical Patients' Satisfaction in Watts." *Health Services Report*, 88 (1973): 351-59. See also: Health, Medicine, and Folk Medicine.

851. McCaslin, R., and Calvert, W. "Social Indicators in Black and White: Some Ethnic Considerations in Delivery of Service to the Elderly." *Journal of Gerontology*, 30, no. 1 (1975): 60-66.

852. Mindel, C. H., and Wright, R. "The Use of Social Services by Black and White Elderly: The Role of Social Support Systems." *Journal of Gerontological Social Work*, 4, no. 3-4 (1982): 107-25.

853. Polansky, G. "Planning for the Specially Disadvantaged Minority Groups: Clinical Experience." In *National Conference on Alternatives to Institutional Care for Older Americans*, ed. by E. Pfeiffer. Durham: Duke University, 1973. See also: Mental Health and Life Satisfaction.

854. Russell, M. "Social Work in A Black Community Hospital." *American Journal of Public Health*, 60 (1970): 704. See also: Health, Medicine, and Folk Medicine.

855. Slaughter, O. W., and Batey, M. O. "Service Delivery and the Black Aged: Identifying Barriers to Utilization of Mental Health Services." In *Minority Aging: Sociological and Social Psychological Issues*, ed. by R. C. Manuel. Westport, Conn.: Greenwood Press, 1982.

856. Solomon, B. "Social and Protective Services." In *Community Services and the Black Elderly*, ed. by R. H. Davis. Los Angeles: The Ethel Percy Andrus Gerontology Center, University of Southern California, 1972.

857. Stanford, E. P. "Excerpts on Black Aged From the Urban News: Community Organizations and Minority Aged." In *Growing Old in America*, ed. by B. B. Hess. New Brunswick: Transaction, 1976.

858. _____. "Service Delivery From a Minority Aged Perspective: The Aged Black." In *Black/Chicano Elderly: Service Delivery Within a Cultural Context*, ed. by R. Wright. Arlington: University of Texas at Arlington, 1980.

859.   Wright, R.; Creecy, R.; and Berg, W. "The Black Elderly and Their
       Use of Health Care Services: A Causal Analysis." *Journal of Geronto-
       logical Social Work*, 2, no. 1 (1979): 11-27. See also: Health, Medicine,
       and Folk Medicine.
See also 411.

Theory, Research, and Training

860.   Beattie, Jr., W. M., and Morgan, H. "Curriculum Development on
       Aged Blacks in Predominantly White Environments." In *Proceedings
       of Black Aged in the Future*, ed. by J. J. Jackson. Durham: Duke Uni-
       versity, 1973.

861.   Dancy, Jr., J. *The Black Elderly: A Manual for Practitioners*. Ann
       Arbor: The Institute of Gerontology, University of Michigan-
       Wayne State University, 1977. See also: Support Services and Ser-
       vice Delivery.

862.   Faris, J. B., ed. "Job Bank Lists Blacks in Field of Aging." *Aging*
       (August 1977): 24a.

863.   Jackson, J. J. "Exhibit A. Negro Aged and Social Gerontology: Cur-
       rent Status and Some Emerging Issues." In *Long-Range Program and
       Research Needs in Aging and Related Fields*. Hearings Before the Special
       Committee on Aging, U.S. Senate, Part I, Survey Dec. 5 & 6, 1967.
       Washington, D.C.: U.S. Government Printing Office, 1967.

864.   _____. "Improving the Training of Health Paraprofessionals."
       In *Mental Health: Principles and Training Techniques in Nursing Home
       Care*, ed. by M. Crumbaugh. Rockville, Md.: National Institute of
       Mental Health, 1972. See also: Mental Health and Life Satisfaction;
       Support Services and Service Delivery.

865.   _____. "The National Center on Black Aged: A Challenge to
       Gerontologists." *Gerontologist*, 14 (1974): 194.

866.   _____. "Negro Aged and Social Gerontology: A Critical Eval-
       uation." *Journal of Social and Behavioral Sciences*, 13 (1968): 42-47.

867.   _____. "Negro Aged: Toward Needed Research in Social Ger-
       ontology." *Gerontologist*, 11, no. 1, pt. 2 (1971): 52-57.

868.   _____. "Social Gerontology and the Negro: A Review." *Ger-
       ontologist*, 7 (1967): 168-78.

869.   Jackson, J. J. and Eisdorfer, C. "Research, Training, Service, and Ac-
       tion Concerns About Black Aging and Aged Persons: An
       Overview." In *Proceedings of the Research Conference on the Minority
       Group Aged in the South*, ed. by J. J. Jackson. Durham: Duke Univer-
       sity, 1972.

870. Jenkins, A. H. "The Aged Black: Some Reflections on the Literature." *Afro-American Studies, 3* (1972): 217-21.

871. Kastenbaum, R. J. "Psychological Research Concerns Relative to Aging and Aged Blacks." In *Proceedings of the Research Conference on the Minority Group Aged in the South,* ed. by J. J. Jackson. Durham: Duke University, 1972.

872. Lindsay, I. and Hawkins, B. "Research Issues Relating to the Black Aged." *Social Research and the Black Community: Selected Issues and Priorities,* ed. by L. Gary. Washington, D.C.: Institute for Urban Affairs and Research, Howard University, 1974.

873. Reed, J. "Prospects for Developing Gerontological Training Programs at Black Institutions." In *Proceedings of the Research Conference on the Minority Group Aged in the South,* ed. by J. J. Jackson. Durham: Duke University, 1972.

874. Sherman, G. A., ed. *Curriculum Guidelines in Minority Aging.* Washington, D.C.: National Center on Black Aged, 1980.

875. _____, ed. *Research and Training in Minority Aging.* Washington, D.C.: National Center on Black Aged, 1978.

876. Smith, S. H. "Social Gerontology." In *Proceedings of the Workshop Series on the Black Aged and Aging,* ed. by J. Dorsett-Robinson. Carbondale: Southern Illinois University, 1974.

877. Stanford, E. P. "Theoretical and Practical Relationships Among Aged Blacks and Other Minorities." *Black Scholar, 13,* no. 1 (1982): 49-57.

878. Staples, R. *Introduction to Black Sociology.* New York: McGraw Hill, 1976.

See also 452, 455, 478, 479, 488.

Women

879. Carson, J. *Silent Voices: The Southern Negro Woman Today.* New York: Dell, 1969.

880. Clarke, J. H. "A Search for Identity." *Social Casework, 51,* no. 5 (1970): 259-64.

881. Daly, F. Y. "To Be Black Poor, Female, & Old." *Freedomways,* 16, no. 4 (1976): 223-29.

882. Gibson, R. C. "Efficacy Changes in Aging and Aged Female Heads of Households: A Black-White Comparison." *International Journal of Aging and Human Development.* Forthcoming.

883.   Jackson, J. J. "Categorical Differences of Older Black Women." *Generations* (August 1980): 17.

884.   _____. "Menopausal Attitudes and Behaviors Among Senescent Black Women and Predictors of Changing Attitudes and Activities Among Aged Blacks." *Black Aging, 1* (August/October 1976): 8-29. See also: Health, Medicine, and Folk Medicine.

885.   _____. "Older Black Women." In *Looking Ahead: A Women's Guide to the Problems and Joys of Growing Older*, ed. by L. E. Troll, J. Israel, and K. Israel. New Jersey: Prentice-Hall, 1977.

886.   _____. "The Plight of Older Black Women in the United States." *The Black Scholar, 7*, no. 7, (1976): 47-54.

887.   Scott, J. and Kivett, V. "The Widowed, Black, Older Adult in the Rural South: Implications for Policy." *Family Relations, 29* (1980): 83-90. See also: Rural.

See also 503.

Work and Retirement

888.   Abbot, J. "Work Experience and Earnings of Middle Aged Black and White Men, 1965-71." *Social Security Bulletin, 43*, no. 12 (1980): 16-34.

889.   Aiken, M., and Ferman, L. "The Social and Political Reactions of Older Negroes to Unemployment." *Phylon, 27* (1966): 333-46. See also: Social Policy and Politics.

890.   Anderson, A. "Excerpts on Black Aged from the Urban League News: Older Workers Vulnerable in Labor Force." In *Growing Old in America*, ed by B. B. Hess. New Brunswick: Transaction, 1976.

891.   Bender, E. G. "Economics and the Aging." In *Proceedings of the Workshop Series on the Black Aged and Aging and the Conference on the Black Aged and Aging*, ed. by J. Dorsett-Robinson. Carbondale: Southern Illinois University, 1974.

892.   Cowan, B. "Urban Blacks in Retirement: Current Status, Prospects and Issues." In *Retirement: Concepts and Realities*, ed. by E. P. Stanford. San Diego: San Diego State University, 1978.

893.   Gillespie, B. J. "Elderly Blacks and the Economy." *The Journal of Afro-American Issues, 3* (1975): 324-35.

894.   Hamilton, R. N. *Employment Needs and Programs for Older Workers— Especially Blacks.* Washington, D.C.: National Center on Black Aged, 1975.

895. Hearn, H. L. "Career and Leisure Patterns of Middle-Aged Urban Blacks." *Gerontologist*, *11*, no. 4, pt. 2 (1971): 21-26. See also: Social Participation and Friendships.

896. Hicks, N. "Retirement: Giving it Five More Years—Who Wins, Who Loses?" *Black Enterprise* (December 1977): 1-9.

897. Jackson, J. J. "Retirement Patterns of Aged Blacks." In *Retirement: Concepts and Realities*, ed. by E. P. Stanford. San Diego: San Diego State University, 1978.

898. Koba Associates, Inc., *Condition Forecast: Economic Security and Productivity Among Black Aged in the Year 2000*. Washington, D.C.: Koba Associates, Inc., 1980.

899. Lambing, M. "Social Class Living Patterns of Retired Negroes." *Gerontologist*, *12*, no. 3 pt. 1 (1972): 285-88. See also: Social Participation and Friendships; Marriage and Family.

900. Mallan, L. "Women Born in the Early 1900's: Employment, Earnings, and Benefit Levels." *Social Security Bullletin*, *37* (March 1974): 3-16. See also: Demographic and Socioeconomic Characteristics; Women.

901. Miles, L. "Midlife Career Change for Blacks: Problems and Issues." *Vocational Guidance Quarterly*, *30*, no. 1 (1981): 5-13.

902. Oliver, M. "Elderly Blacks and the Economy." *Journal of Afro-American Issues*, *3* (1975): 316-23.

903. Snyder, D. C. "Future Pension Status of the Black Elderly." In *Ethnicity and Aging: Theory, Research and Policy*, ed. by D. E. Gelfand and A. J. Kutzik. New York: Springer, 1979. See also: Demographic and Socioeconomic Characteristics.

904. Thompson, G. B. "Black-White Differences in Private Pensions: Findings from the Retirement History Study." *Social Security Bulletin*, *42* (1979): 15-40. See also: Demographic and Socioeconomic Characteristics.

905. Wallace, E. C. "Retirement Income for the Black Elderly." In *Minority Aging: Policy Issues for the '80's*, ed. by E. P. Stanford. San Diego: San Diego State University, 1980. See also: Demographic and Socioeconomic Characteristics.

See also 515.

III. HISPANIC AMERICANS

Death and Dying

906. Fierro, A. "A Note on Death and Dying." *Hispanic Journal of Behavioral Sciences, 2*, no. 4 (1980): 401-6.

907. Markides, K. S. "Death-Related Attitudes and Behavior Among Mexicans: A Review." *Suicide and Life-Threatening Behavior, 11*, no. 2 (1981): 75-85.

908. Markides, K. S., and Pappas, C. "Subjective Age, Health, and Survivorship in Old Age." *Research on Aging, 4*, no. 1 (1982): 87-96. See also: Health, Medicine, and Folk Medicine.

909. Moore, J. W. "The Death Culture of Mexico and Mexican Americans." *Omega, 1* (1970): 271-91.

910. Reynolds, D., and Kalish, R. "The Meaning of Death and Dying in the Los Angeles Mexican-American Community." In *Proceedings of International Association for Suicide Prevention*, Mexico City, 1971.

Demographic and Socioeconomic Characteristics

911. Atencio, T. "Advocacy Through Popular Education." In *Proceedings of the National Conference on Spanish-Speaking Elderly*, ed. by A. Hernandez and J. Mendoza. Kansas City: National Chicano Planning Council, 1975. See also: Social Policy and Politics.

912. Bardsley and Haslacker, Inc. *Profile of the Latin Adults in Dade County and the Households They Live In*. Palo Alto, California: October 1967. See also: Housing.

913. Clark, J. M. "Los Cubanos de Miami: Cuantos Son y de Donde Provienen." *Ideal* (Miami) (January 15, 1973).

914. _____. "Donde Viven los Cubanos?" Caracteristicas Residenciales de los Cubanos de Miami-Dade." *Ideal* (Miami) (February 15, 1973). See also: Housing.

915. Estrada, L. "The Spanish Origin Elderly: A Demographic Survey, 1970-1975." *Texas Department of Public Welfare, Research Utilization Report for the Aging, 4* (1977): 13-14.

916. Federation of Experienced Americans and U.S. Human Resources Corporation. *The Spanish-Speaking Elderly Poor. Part 1. The Assessment of Demographic Data and Recommendations for the Establishment of a National Information Center and Three Prototype Centers*. Washington, D.C. and San Francisco, California, n.d. See also: Support Services and Service Delivery.

917. Mendoza, M., and Clark, J. "Characteristics and Needs of the Spanish-Speaking Elderly in Dade County." In *The Cuban Minority in the U.S.: Final Report on Need Identification and Program Evaluation.* Washington, D.C.: Cuban National Planning Council, 1974.

918. Mittelbach, F., and Marshall, G. *Mexican-American Study Project Advanced Report, No. 5. The Burden of Poverty.* Los Angeles: School of Business Administration, July, 1966.

919. Newman, M. "A Profile of Hispanics in the U.S. Work Force" *Monthly Labor Review* (December 1978): 3-14.

920. Ramirez, H. M. "America's Spanish-Speaking—A Profile." *Manpower* (September 1972.) See also: Work and Retirement.

921. Teller, C.; Estrada, L.; Hernandez, J.; and Alvirez, D., eds. *Cuantos Somos: A Demographic Study of the Mexican-American Population.* Austin: Center for Mexican American Studies, University of Texas, 1977.

922. U.S. Bureau of the Census. "Census of Population: 1960. Supplementary Reports." *Population Characteristics of Selected Ethnic Groups in the Five Southwestern States.* Series PC (S-1)-55. Washington, D.C.: U.S. Government Printing Office, 1968.

923. _____. Census of Population: 1970. Subject Reports." *Persons of Spanish Origin.* Final Report PC (2)-1C Washington, D.C.: U.S Government Printing Office, 1973.

924. _____. "Current Population Reports." *Persons of Spanish Origin in the United States: March, 1976.* Series P-20, no. 302. Washington, D.C.: U.S. Government Printing Office, 1976.

925. White House Conference on Aging (1971). "Educational Problems of Spanish-Speaking Elderly." Washington, D.C.: U.S. Government Printing Office, 1971.

926. _____. "Points of Discussion on Income Problems of Elderly Mexican-Americans." Washington, D.C.: U.S. Government Printing Office, 1971.
See also 30.

General

927. Anson, R. "Hispanics in the United States: Yesterday, Today, and Tomorrow." *Futurist, 14* (1980): 25-32.

928.   Aranda, R. G. "The Mexican-American Syndrome." *American Journal of Public Health and the Nation's Health*, 61, no. 1 (1971): 104-9.

929.   Burma, J. M., ed. *Mexican-Americans in the United States: A Reader.* Cambridge: Schenkman, 1970.

930.   Cabinet Committee on Opportunities for Spanish-Speaking People. *Spanish-Speaking Elderly: A Working Paper for the White House*, 1973.

931.   Clark, M., and Mendelson, M. "Mexican-American Aged in San Francisco: A Case Description." *Gerontologist*, 9, no. 2; pt. 1 (1969): 90-95.

932.   Coles, R. C. *The Old Ones of New Mexico.* Albuquerque: University of New Mexico Press, 1974.

933.   _____. *Una Anciana.* In *Growing Old in America*, ed. B. B. Hess. New Brunswick: Transaction Books, 1976.

934.   Donaldson, E., and Martinez, E. "The Hispanic Elderly of East Harlem." *Aging*, 6 (1980): 305-6.

935.   Eribes, R. A. "The Older Mexican American: The Invisible Elderly." *Aztlan*, 10 (Spring/Fall, 1979): 91-100.

936.   Hernandez, A., and Mendoza, J., eds. *Proceedings of the National Conference on the Spanish-Speaking Elderly.* Kansas City: National Chicano Social Planning Council, 1975.

937.   Hernandez, J. J. "Old, Alone, and Forgotten." *Nuestro* (1977).

938.   Hill, A. O. *A Study of Michigan's Chicano Population.* Ann Arbor: Institute of Gerontology, University of Michigan, 1971.

939.   La Luz. "The Hispano Aged." *La Luz*, 7, no. 3 (1975): entire issue.

940.   Lecca, P. J. "Puerto Rican Perspective: Latino Enigma — Similarities and Differences." In *Proceedings of the National Conference on Spanish-Speaking Elderly*, ed. by A. Hernandez and J. Mendoza. Kansas City: National Chicano Planning Council, 1975.

941.   Maldonado, D. "Aging in the Chicano Context." In *Ethnicity and Aging: Theory, Research and Policy*, ed. by D. Gelfand and A. Kutzik. New York: Springer, 1979.

942.   _____. "The Chicano Aged." *Social Work*, 20, no. 3 (1975): 213-16.

943.   _____. "The Ethnic Minority Elderly: The Case of the Mexican American." In *Black/Chicano Elderly: Service Delivery Within A Cultural Context*, ed. by R. Wright. Arlington: Graduate School of Social Work, University of Texas at Arlington, 1980.

944. Manrique, J. P. "Cuban Perspective." In *The National Conference on Spanish-Speaking Elderly*, ed. by A. Hernandez and J. Mendoza. Kansas City: National Chicano Social Planning Council, 1975.

945. Markides, K. S., "Ethnic Differences in Age Identification: A Study of Older Mexican Americans and Anglos." *Social Science Quarterly*, 60 (1980): 659-66.

946. Markides, K. S., and Martin, H. W. with the assistance of E. Gomez. *Older Mexican Americans: A Study in an Urban Barrio*. Austin: Center for Mexican American Studies, University of Texas Press, 1983.

947. Martinez, H. *The Mexican-American Elderly*. Washington, D.C.: National Council on the Aging, 1971.

948. Miranda, M. "Latin American Culture and American Society: Contrasts." In *The National Conference on Spanish-Speaking Elderly*, ed. by A. Hernandez and J. Mendoza. Kansas City: National Chicano Social Planning Council, 1975.

949. Moore, J. W. "Mexican Americans." *Gerontologist*, 11 (1971): 30-35.

950. National Association for Spanish-Speaking Elderly. *Search for Hispanic Models, Final Report*. Los Angeles: The First Western Regional Conference on Aging, 1976.

951. Reich, J. M.; Stegman, M. A; and Stegman, N. W.; *Relocating the Dispossessed Elderly: A Study of Mexican Americans*. Philadelphia: University of Pennsylvania, Institute of Environmental Studies, 1966.

952. Reyes, M. *Elderly Cubans in Exile*. Working Paper prepared for the Special Committee on Aging, U.S. Senate. Washington, D.C.: U.S. Government Printing Office, 1971.

953. Ruiz, F. "Chicano Perspective." In *The National Conference on the Spanish-Speaking Elderly*, ed. by A. Hernandez and J. Mendoza. Kansas City: National Chicano Social Planning Council, 1975.

954. Samora, J. and Lamanna, R. A. *Mexican-Americans in a Midwest Metropolis: A Study of East Chicago*. Los Angeles: UCLA Graduate School of Business Administration, Mexican-American Study Project, Advance Report 8, 1967.

955. Sanchez, P. "The Spanish Heritage Elderly." In *Minority Aging: Institute on Minority Aging Proceedings*, ed. by E. P. Stanford. San Diego: San Diego State University, 1974.

956.   Sotomayor, M. "Social Change and the Spanish-Speaking Elderly." In *The National Conference on the Spanish-Speaking Elderly*, ed. by A. Hernandez and K. Mendoza. Kansas City: National Chicano Social Planning Council, 1975.

957.   Szapocznik, J., and Kurtines, W. "Acculturation, Biculturalism and Adjustment Among Cuban Americans." In *Acculturation: Theory, Models and Some New Findings*, ed. by A. M. Padilla. Boulder, Colorado: Westview Press, 1980.

958.   Torres-Gil, F. "Concerns of the Spanish-Speaking Elderly." In *Minority Aging: Second Institute on Minority Aging Proceedings*, ed. by E. P. Stanford. San Diego: San Diego State University, 1975.

959.   U.S. Senate, Special Committee on Aging. "Elderly Cubans in Exile: A Working Paper." Washington, D.C.: U.S. Government Printing Office 1971.

960.   Valle, R., and Mendoza L., *The Elder Latino*. San Diego: San Diego State Univiersity, 1978.

961.   White House Conference on Aging. *Reports of the Special Concern Sessions, 1971: The Spanish-Speaking Elderly*. Washington, D.C.: U.S. Government Printing Office, 1971.

962.   _____. "The Spanish-Speaking Elderly." *Toward a National Policy on Aging*. Washington, D.C.: U.S. Government Printing Office, 1971.

963.   Wilson, H., and Heinert, J. "Los Viejitos: The Old Ones." *Journal of Gerontological Nursing*, 3, no. 5 (1977): 19-27.
See also 6, 279.

Health, Medicine, and Folk Medicine

964.   Cervantes, R. A. "Urban Chicanos: Failure of Comprehensive Health Services." *Health Service Reports*, 87 (1972): 932-40. See also: Support Services and Service Delivery.

965.   Clark, M. *Health in the Mexican-American Culture*. Berkeley: University of California Press, 1959.

966.   Davis, R. H., ed. *Health Services and the Mexican-American Elderly*. Los Angeles: The Ethel Percy Andrus Gerontology Center, University of Southern California, 1973. See also: Support Services and Service Delivery.

967.   Delgado, M. "Herbal Medicine in the Puerto Rican Community." *Health and Social Work*, 4 (1979): 24-40.

968. East Los Angeles Health System, Inc. *East Los Angeles Health: Supplemental Report on Health Problems and Priorities in East Los Angeles.* Los Angeles: East Los Angeles Health Task Force, University of Southern California School of Medicine, 1972.

969. Edgerton, R; Karno, M; and Fernandez, I. "Curanderismo in the Metropolis: The Diminished Role of Folk Psychiatry Among Los Angeles Mexican-Americans." *American Journal of Psychotherapy, 24,* no. 1 (1970): 124-34. See also: Mental Health and Life Satisfaction.

970. Eribes, R., and Bradley-Rawls, M. "Underutilization of Nursing-Home Facilities by Mexican American Elderly in the Southwest." *Gerontologist, 18* (1978): 363-71.

971. Hill, A. O. "Vital Health Concerns." In *The National Conference on the Spanish-Speaking Elderly,* ed. by A. Hernandez and J. Mendoza. Kansas City: National Chicano Social Planning Council, 1975.

972. Kiev, A. *Curanderismo: Mexican-American Folk Psychiatry.* New York: Free Press, 1968.

973. Markides, K. S., and Martin, H. "Predicting Self-Rated Health Among the Aged." *Research on Aging, 1* (1979): 97-112.

974. Markides, K. S., and Pappas, C. "Subjective Age, Health and Survivorship in Old Age." *Research on Aging, 4* (1982): 87-93.

975. Menck, H. R.; Henderson, B. E.; Pike, M. C.; Mack, T.; Martin, S. P.; and SooHoo, J. "Cancer Incidence in the Mexican-American." *Journal of the National Cancer Institute, 55,* no. 3 (1975): 531-36.

976. Mexican-American Policy Research Project. *The Health of Mexican Americans in South Texas:* Austin: LBJ School of Public Affairs, University of Texas, 1979.

977. Moustafa, A., and Weiss, G. *Health Status and Practices of Mexican Americans.* Los Angeles: University of California at Los Angeles, Mexican American Study Project, Advance Report 11, 1968.

978. Newton, F. "The Hispanic Elderly: A Review of Health, Social, and Psychological Factors." In *Explorations in Chicano Psychology,* ed. by A. Baron. New York: Praeger, 1981. See also: Mental Health and Life Satisfaction.

979. Ramirez, A.; Herrick, K.; and Weaver, F. "El Asesino Silencioso: A Methodology for Alerting the Spanish-Speaking Community." *Urban Health* (June 1981): 44-48.

980. Rubel, A. J. *Across the Tracks: Mexican-Americans in a Texas City* [Hidalgo County, Texas]. Austin: University of Texas Press, 1966. See also: Mental Health and Life Satisfaction.

981. _____. "Concepts of Disease in Mexican American Culture."
     American Anthropologist, 62 (1960): 795-814.

982. Salcido, R. "Health Advocacy for Mexican American Seniors." *The
     Borderlands Journal,* 4, no. 1 (1980): 87.

983. _____. "Needed: Hypertension Research for Mexican-Ameri-
     cans." *Public Health Reports,* 94 (1979): 371-76. See also: Theory,
     Research, and Training.

984. Sanchez, R., and Bynum, G. "Health Care in Rural New Mexico."
     Journal of Medical Health Care, 48 (1973): 124-29.

985. Saunders, L. *Cultural Differences and Medical Care: The Case of the
     Spanish-Speaking People of the Southwest.* New York: Russell Sage,
     1954.

986. Stern, M.; Haskell, W.; and Wood, P. "Affluence and Cardiovascular
     Risk Factors in Mexican-American and other Whites in Three North-
     ern California Communities." *Journal of Chronic Diseases,* 28 (1975):
     623-36.

987. Stern, M., and Gaskill, S. "Secular Trends in Ischemic Heart Disease
     and Stroke Mortality from 1970 to 1976 in Spanish-Surnamed and
     Other White Individuals in Bexar County, Texas" *Circulation,* 58
     (1978): 537-43. See also: Mortality.

988. Torres-Gil, F. M. "Age, Health, and Culture: An Examination of
     Health among Spanish-Speaking Elderly." In *Hispanic Families: Criti-
     cal Issues for Policy and Programs in Human Services,* ed by M. Montiel.
     Washington, D.C.: National Coalition of Hispanic Mental Health
     and Human Service Organizations, 1978.

989. Trotter, R. T., and Chavira, J. A. *Curanderismo: Mexican American
     Folk Healing.* Athens: University of Georgia Press, 1981.

990. Vega, W. "Defining Hispanic High Risk Groups: Targeting Popula-
     tions for Health Promotion." In *Hispanic Support Systems: Mental
     Health Promotion Perspectives,* ed. by R. Valle and W. Vega. Sacra-
     mento: State of California Department of Mental Health, 1980.

991. Vener, A. M; Krupka, L. R; and Climo, J. J. "Drug Usage and
     Health Characteristics in Noninstitutionalized Mexican-American
     Elderly." *Journal of Drug Education,* 10, no. 4 (1980): 343-53.

992. Weclew, R. V. "The Nature, Prevalence and Level of Awareness of
     'Curanderismo' and Some of its Implications for Community Mental
     Health." *Community Mental Health Journal,* 11 (1975): 145-54.

993. Welch, S.; Comer, J.; and Steinman, M. "Some Social and Attitudinal Correlates of Health Care Among Mexican Americans." *Journal of Health and Social Behavior, 14* (1973): 205-13. See also: Mental Health and Life Satisfaction.

994. Zambrana, R.; Merino, R.; and Santana, S. "Health Services and the Puerto Rican Elderly." In *Ethnicity and Aging: Theory, Research and Policy*, ed. by D. E. Gelfand and A. J. Kutzik. New York: Springer, 1979. See also: Support Services and Service Delivery.
See also 141, 153, 160.

Housing

995. Carp, F. *A Future for the Aged: The Residents of Victoria Plaza*. Austin: University of Texas Press, 1966.

996. _____. "Housing and Minority Group Elderly." *Gerontologist, 9* (1969): 20-24.

997. _____. "Some Determinants of Low Application Rates of Mexican-Americans for Public Housing for the Elderly." Hearings before the Special Committee on Aging, U.S. Senate. Washington, D.C.: U.S. Government Printing Office, 1969. See also: Support Services and Service Delivery.

998. Echeverria, D. "Housing Problems of the Spanish-American Elderly." In *The National Conference on the Spanish Speaking Elderly*, ed. by A. Hernandez and J. Mendoza. Kansas City: National Chicano Social Planning Council, 1975.

999. Mendoza, M. G. *Housing Conditions of Cubans, Puerto Ricans, and Mexicans in Dade County, Florida*. Washington, D.C.: U.S. Department of HUD, April 19, 1974.

1000. White House Conference on Aging, 1971. "The Mexican-American Elderly's Special Problems With Federally Subsidized Housing." Washington, D.C.: U.S. Government Printing Office, 1971.
See also 177.

Marriage and Family

1001. Alvirez, D.; Bean, F.; and Williams, D. "The Mexican American Family." In *Ethnic Families in America*. 2d ed., ed. by C. H. Mindel and R. W. Habenstein. New York: Elsevier, 1981.

1002. Angel, R., and Tienda, M. "Determinants of Extended Household Structure: Cultural Pattern or Economic Need?" *American Journal of Sociology, 87* (May 1982): 1360-83. See also: Demographic and Socioeconomic Characteristics.

1003. Bastida, E. "Family Integration in Later Life Among Hispanic Americans." *Journal of Minority Aging*, 4 (1979): 42-49.

1004. Fitzpatrick, J. P. "The Puerto Rican Family." In *Ethnic Families in America*, 2d ed., ed. by C. H. Mindel and R. W. Habenstein. New York: Elsevier, 1981.

1005. Gonzalez, M., and Garcia, D. "A Study of Extended Family Interactions Among Chicanos in the East Los Angeles Area." *Chicano Studies Documents, Research Projects, and Resources*. Los Angeles: University of California at Los Angeles, 1974.

1006. Maldonado, D. "La Familia Mexico Americana and the Elderly." *Research Utilization Report for the Aging of the Texas Department of Public Welfare*, 4, no. 9 (1977): 9, 18.

1007. Martinez, M. A. "Family Policy for Mexican Americans and Their Aged." *Urban and Social Change Review*, 12, no. 2 (1979): 16-19.

1008. Martinez, M. Z. "The Mexican American Family: A Weakened Support System?" In *Minority Aging: Policy Issues for the '80's*, ed. by E. P. Stanford. San Diego: San Diego State University, 1980. See also: Support Services and Service Delivery.

1009. Miranda, M. "The Family Natural Support System in Hispanic Communities: Preliminary Research Notes and Recommendations." In *Hispanic Support Systems: Mental Health Promotion Perspectives*, ed. by R. Valle and W. Vega. Sacramento: State of California Department of Mental Health, 1980. See also: Support Services and Service Delivery.

1010. Montiel, M. "The Chicano Family: A Review of Research." *Social Work* (March 1973): 22-31. See also: Theory, Research, and Training.

1011. _____. "The Mexican American Family: A Proposed Research Framework." In *The National Conference on Spanish-Speaking Elderly*, ed. by A. Hernandez and J. Mendoza. Kansas City: National Chicano Social Planning Council, 1975. See also: Theory, Research, and Training.

1012. Samora, J., and Larson, R. "Rural [Mexican American] Families in an Urban Setting: A Study in Persistence and Change." *Journal of Human Relations*, 9 (1961): 494-503. See also: Rural.
See also 194.

Mental Health and Life Satisfaction

1013. Acosta, M. R. "Ethnic Adaptation by the Hispanic Elderly." *La Luz*, 4, no. 4 (1975): 24-25. See also: Social Participation and Friendships.

1014. Bachrach, L. "Utilization of State and County Mental Hospitals by Spanish Americans in 1972." Washington, D.C.: National Institute of Mental Health, 1975. See also: Support Services and Service Delivery.

1015. Baron, Jr., A., ed. *Explorations in Chicano Psychology.* New York: Praeger, 1981.

1016. Edgerton, R., and Karno, M. "Mexican-American Bilingualism and the Perception of Mental Illness." *Archives of General Psychiatry, 24* (1971): 286-90.

1017. Fabrega, H.; Rubel, A.; and Wallace, C. "Working Class Mexican Psychiatric Outpatients: Some Social and Cultural Features." *Archives of General Psychiatry, 16* (1967): 704-12.

1018. Gaitz, C., and Scott, J. "Mental Health of Mexican-Americans: Do Ethnic Factors Makes a Difference?" *Geriatrics, 29* (1974): 103-10.

1019. Gomez, E.; Martin, H.; and Gibson, G. "Adaptation of Older Mexican-Americans: Some Implications for Social and Health Problems." In *Emerging Perspectives on Chicano Mental Health,* Monograph No. 1. Houston: Chicano Training Center, 1975. See also: Health, Medicine, and Folk Medicine.

1020. Haberman, P. W. "Ethnic Differences in Psychiatric Symptoms Reported in Community Surveys." *Public Health Reports, 85,* no. 6 (1970): 495-502.

1021. Karno, M.; Ross, R.; and Caper, R. "Mental Health Role of Physicians in a Mexican-American Community." *Community Mental Health Journal, 5* (1969): 62-69. See also: Health, Medicine, and Folk Medicine.

1022. Karno, M., and Edgerton, R. "Perception of Mental Illness in a Mexican-American Community." *Archives of General Psychiatry, 20* (1969): 233-38.

1023. Korte, A. O. "Social Interaction and Morale of Spanish-Speaking Rural and Urban Elderly." *Journal of Gerontological Social Work, 4,* nos. 3-4 (Spring, Summer 1982): 57-66. See also: Social Participation and Friendships; Rural.

1024. _____. "Theoretical Perspectives in Mental Health and the Mexicano Elders." In *Chicano Aging and Mental Health,* ed. by M. Miranda and R. Ruiz. U.S. Department of Health and Human Services, 1981. See also: Theory, Research, and Training.

1025. Markides, K. S. "Correlates of Life Satisfaction Among Older Mexican Americans and Anglos." *Journal of Minority Aging*, 5, no. 2: (1980): 183-90.

1026. Markides, K. S.; Costley, D.; and Rodriguez, L. "Perceptions of Intergenerational Relations and Psychological Well-Being Among Elderly Mexican Americans: A Causal Model." *International Journal of Aging and Human Development*, 13, no. 1 (1981): 43-52. See also: Marriage and Family.

1027. Markides, K. S.; Martin, H.; and Sizemore, M. "Psychological Distress Among Elderly Mexican Americans and Anglos." *Ethnicity*, 7, no. 3 (1980): 298-309.

1028. Martin, H., and Gomez, E. "Adaptations of Older Mexican-Americans: Some Preliminary Findings." *Research Utilization Report of the Texas State Department of Public Welfare*, 1 (1974): 6-7. See also: Social Participation and Friendships.

1029. Miranda, M., and Ruiz, R., eds. *Chicano Aging and Mental Health.* U.S. Department of Health and Human Services, 1981. See also: Theory, Research, and Training.

1030. Montiel, M. "Social Research and the Chicano Community." In *Chicano Aging and Mental Health*, ed. by M. Miranda and R. Ruiz. U.S. Department of Health and Human Services, 1981. See also: Theory, Research, and Training.

1031. Morales, A. *Distinguishing Psychodynamic Factors From Cultural Factors in the Treatment of the Spanish-Speaking Patient.* Rosemead, California: The Psychiatric Bulletin of the Gilfillan Clinic, 1967.

1032. _____. "Mental and Public Health Issues: The Case of Mexican Americans in Los Angeles." *El Grito*, 3 (1970): 3-11. See also: Health, Medicine, and Folk Medicine.

1033. Newton, F., and Ruiz, R. "Chicano Culture and Mental Health Among the Elderly." In *Chicano Aging and Mental Health*, ed. by M. Miranda and R. Ruiz. U.S. Department of Health and Human Services, 1981. See also: Marriage and Family.

1034. Padilla, A.; Ruiz, R.; and Alvarez, R. "Delivery of Community Mental Health Services to the Spanish-Speaking/Surnamed Population." In *Delivery of Services for Latino Community Mental Health*, ed. by R. Alvarez. Los Angeles: Spanish-Speaking Mental Health Research Center, University of California, 1975. See also: Support Services and Service Delivery.

1035. Padilla, A., and Ruiz, R. *Latino Mental Health—A Review of the Literature.* Rockville, Md.: National Institute of Mental Health, Department of Health, Education, and Welfare, 1975.

1036. Ruiz, R., and Olmedo, E. "The Identification of Mental Health Research Priorities for the Hispanic Elderly in the United States." *Research Bulletin, No. 2.* Los Angeles: Spanish-Speaking Mental Health Research Center, University of California, 1977. See also: Theory, Research, and Training.

1037. Ruiz, R., and Miranda, M. "A Priority List of Research Questions on Mental Health of Chicano Elderly." In *Chicano Aging and Mental Health*, ed. by M. Miranda and R. Ruiz. U.S. Department of Health and Human Services, 1981. See also: Theory, Research, and Training.

1038. Santos, R. "Aging and Chicano Mental Health: An Economic Perspective." In *Chicano Aging and Mental Health*, ed. by. M. Miranda and R. Ruiz. U.S. Department of Health and Human Services, 1981. See also: Demographic and Socioeconomic Characteristics.

1039. Sotomayor, M.; Zapata, C.; and Garza, B. "Mental Health Among the Elderly in the Barrio." *Agenda* 7 (1977): 32-35.

1040. Szapocznik, J. "A Programmatic Mental Health Approach to Enhancing the Meaning of Life of Cuban Elderly." In *Hispanic Report on Families and Youth.* Washington, D.C.: COSSMHO, 1980.

1041. Szapocznik, J.; Faletti, M.; and Scopetta, M. "Psychological-Social Issues of Cuban Elders in Miami." In *Cuban Americans: Acculturation, Adjustment and the Family*, ed. by J. Szapocznik and M. Herrera. Washington, D.C.: COSSMHO, 1979.

1042. Szapocznik, J.; Lasaga, J.; Perry, P.; and Solomon, J. "Outreach in the Delivery of Mental Health Services to Hispanic Elders." *Hispanic Journal of Behavioral Sciences*, 1, no. 1 (March, 1979): 21-40. See also: Support Services and Service Delivery.

1043. Szapocznik, J.; Santisteban, D.; Kurtines, W.; and Hervis, O. "'Life Enhancement Couseling for Hispanic Elders." *Aging* (March-April 1980): 20-29.

1044. Szapocznik, J.; Santisteban, D.; Kurtines, W.; Hervis, O.; and Spencer, F. "Life Enhancement Counseling: A Psychosocial Model of Services for Cuban Elders." In *Minority Mental Health*, ed. by E. Jones and S. Korchin. New York: Holt, Rinehart and Winston, 1980. See also: Support Services and Service Delivery.

1045. Szapocznik, J.; Santisteban, D.; Hervis, O.; Spencer, F.; and Kurtines, W. "Treatment of Depression Among Cuban American Elders: Some Validational Evidence for Life Enhancement Counseling Approach." *Journal of Consulting and Clinical Psychology*, 49, no. 5 (1981): 752-54.

1046. Valle, R., and Martinez, C. "Natural Networks of Elderly Latinos of Mexican Heritage: Implications for Mental Health." In *Chicano Aging and Mental Health*, ed. by M. Miranda and R. Ruiz. U.S. Department of Health and Human Services, 1981.

1047. Valle, R., and Vega, W., eds. *Hispanic Support Systems: Mental Health Promotion Perspectives.* Sacramento: State of California Department of Mental Health, 1980. See also: Support Services and Service Delivery.

See also 219, 227.

Mortality

1048. Bradshaw, B., and Fonner, E. "The Mortality of Spanish-Surnamed Persons in Texas: 1969-1971." In *The Demography of Racial and Ethnic Groups*, ed. by F. Bean and W. P. Frisbie. New York: Academic, 1978.

1049. Ellis, J. "Mortality Differences for Spanish-Surname Population Group." *Southwestern Social Science Quarterly*, 39 (1959): 314-21.

1050. _____. "Spanish-Surname Mortality Differences in San Antonio, Texas." *Journal of Health and Human Behavior*, 3 (1962): 125-217.

1051. Eribes, R. A., and Bradley-Rawls, M. "The Underutilization of Nursing Home Facilities by Mexican American Elderly in the Southwest." *Gerontologist*, 18 (1978): 363-71.

1052. Markides, K. S. "Aging, Religiosity and Adjustment: A Longitudinal Analysis. " *Journal of Gerontology*, 38 (1983): 621-25.

1053. Roberts, R. "The Study of Mortality in the Mexican-American Population." In *Cuantos Somos: A Demographic Study of the Mexican-American Population*, ed. by C. Teller, L. Estrada, J. Hernandez, and D. Alvirez. Austin: Center for Mexican American Studies, University of Texas, 1977.

1054. Shoen, R., and Nelson, V. "Mortality by Cause Among Spanish-Surnamed Californians, 1969-1971." *Social Science Quarterly*, 62 (1981): 259-74. See also: Health, Medicine, and Folk Medicine.

1055. U.S. Bureau of the Census. *Coverage of the Hispanic Population of the United States in the 1970 Census.* Current Population Reports. Special Studies, Series P-23, no. 82. Washington, D.C.: U.S. Government Printing Office, 1980.

See also 247, 252.

Rural

1056. Leonard, O. E. "The Older Rural Spanish-Speaking People of the Southwest." In *Older Rural Americans*, ed. by E. G. Youmans. Lexington: University of Kentucky Press, 1967.

1057. Mendoza, L. "Minority Aging Populations: Rural vs. Urban Concentrations—Tapping into the Networks in Process." In *Minority Aging Research: Old Issues—New Approaches*, ed. by. E. P. Stanford. San Diego: San Diego State University, 1979. See also: Demographic and Socioeconomic Characteristics.

Social Participation and Friendships

1058. Cuellar, J. B. "El Senior Citizen's Club: The Older Mexican American in the Vountary Association." In *Life's Career—Aging: Subcultural Variations in Growing Old*, ed. by B. G. Myerhoff and A. Simic. Beverly Hills: Sage, 1978.

1059. _____. "La Ultima Patada: The Impact of Age-Graded Voluntary Associations on Older Members of an Urban Chicano Community." In *Life's Career—Aging: Cross Cultural Studies in Growing Old*, ed. by B. G. Myerhoff and A. Simic. Beverly Hills: Sage, 1978.
See also 295.

Social Policy and Politics

1060. Crawford, J. K. "Analysis of the 'Human Service Model' in Terms of Older Hispanics." In *Understanding Minority Aging: Perspectives and Sources*, ed. by J. B. Cuellar, E. P. Stanford, and D. I. Miller-Soule. San Diego: San Diego State University, 1982.

1061. Cuellar, J. "Aging and Political Realities." In *The National Conference on the Spanish-Speaking Elderly*, ed. by A. Hernandez and J. Mendoza. Kansas City: National Chicano Social Planning Council, 1975.

1062. Donaldson, E., and Martinez, E. "The Hispanic Elderly of East Harlem." *Aging* (March-April 1980): 6-11.

1063. Hernandez, A. "Advocacy and the Neglected Anciano." *Texas Department of Public Welfare, Research Utilization Report for the Aging, 4* (1977): 7-8.

1064. Santiestevan, S. "In Double Jeopardy: The Nation's Aging Hispanics." In *Hispanics and Grantmakers: A Special Report of Foundation News*. Washington, D.C.: Council on Foundations, Inc., 1981.

1065. Torres-Gil, F. *Politics of Aging among Elder Hispanics*. Lanham, Maryland: University Press of America, 1983.

1066. Torres-Gil, F. and Becerra, R. "The Political Behavior of the Mexican-American Elderly." *Gerontologist*, 17, no. 5 (1977): 392-99.

1067. Torres-Gil, F. and Negm, M. "Policy Issues Concerning the Hispanic Elderly." *Aging* (March-April 1980): 2-5.

1068. Torres-Mozqueda, M. "Are There Government Funding Sources Available to Hispanic Senior Citizens?" *Somos*, 1, no. 5 (1978): 48-50.

1069. Velez, C. "The Aged and the Political Process." In *Institute on Aging: An Orientation for Mexican-American Community Workers in the Field of Aging*, ed. by A. Hernandez and J. Mendoza. Kansas City: National Chicano Social Planning Council, 1973.

1070. Velez, C.; Verdugo, R.; and Nunez, F. "Politics and Mental Health Among Elderly Mexicanos." In *Chicano Aging and Mental Health*, ed. by M. Miranda and R. Ruiz. U.S. Department of Health and Human Services, 1981. See also: Mental Health and Life Satisfaction.

Social Security and Old Age Assistance

1071. Schmulowitz, J. "Spanish-Surnamed OASDI Beneficiaries in the Southwest." *Social Security Bulletin*, 36 (1973): 33-36.

1072. Stepanovich, G. "Social Security Beneficiaries With Spanish Surnames in the Southwest." *Social Security Bulletin*, 39 (1976): 48-53.

1073. U.S. Department of Health, Education, and Welfare, Social Security Administration, Office of Research and Statistics. *Spanish-Surnamed Social Security Beneficiaries in the Southwest*. Research and Statistical Note, #28. Washington, D.C.: HEW, 1972.

1074. Weise, R. W. "Recent Changes in Mexican Social Security." *Social Security Bulletin*, 34 (1971): 43-45.

Support Services and Service Delivery

1075. Ahuero, M. "How Can Senior Programs Serve the Public Better?" *Somos*, 1 (1978): 37-38.

1076. Almendarez, M. L. "Analysis of Staff Training Needs in the Delivery of Human Services to the Chicano Elderly in the Metroplex." In *Black/Chicano Elderly: Service Delivery Within A Cultural Context*, ed. by R. Wright. Arlington, Texas: Graduate School of Social Work, University of Texas at Arlington, 1980. See also: Theory, Research, and Training.

1077. Alvarez, R., ed. *Delivery of Services for Latino Community Mental Health*. Los Angeles: Spanish-Speaking Mental Health Research Center, University of California, 1975.

1078. Asociacion Nacional Pro Personas Mayores. *White House Mini-Conference on Hispanic Aging: Final Report.* Los Angeles: Asociacion Nacional Pro Personas Mayores, 1981.

1079. Asociacion Nacional Pro Personas Mayores. "Program Planning and Research for the Hispanic Elderly: A Call for Action." *Final Report on the Second National Hispanic Conference on Aging, 1977.* See also: Theory, Research, and Training.

1080. Carp, F. *Factors in Utilization of Services by the Mexican American Elderly.* Palo Alto: American Institutes for Research, 1968.

1081. Cartwright, W.; Steglich, W.; and Crouch, B. "Use of Community Resources Among Aged Mexican Americans." *Proceedings of the Southwestern Sociological Association, 19* (1969): 184-88.

1082. Crouch, B. M. "Age and Institutional Support: Perceptions of Older Mexican-Americans." *Journal of Gerontology, 27* (1972): 524-29.

1083. Cuellar, J. B. "Conditions of Hispanic Elderly: Intervention and Service Delivery." In *Curriculum Guidelines in Minority Aging,* ed. by G. A. Sherman. Washington, D.C.: National Center on the Black Aged, Inc., 1980.

1084. _____. "Service Delivery and Mental Health Services for Chicano Elders." In *Chicano Aging and Mental Health,* ed. by M. Miranda and R. Ruiz. U.S. Department of Health and Human Services, 1981. See also: Mental Health and Life Satisfaction.

1085. Dieppa, I. "Availability and Usefulness of Federal Programs and Services to Elderly Mexican-Americans: Problems and Prospects." Washington, D.C.: U.S. Senate Special Committee on Aging, U.S. Government Printing Office, 1969.

1086. Lacayo, C. G. "The Asociacion Nacional Pro Personas Mayores: Responding to the Decade of the Hispanic."*Aging* (March-April 1980): 12-13.

1087. _____. *A National Study to Assess the Service Needs of the Hispanic Elderly: Final Report.* Los Angeles: Asociacion Nacional Pro Personas Mayores, 1980.

1088. _____. "Needs Assessment in Minority Aging Research: The Case of the Hispanic Elderly." In *Minority Aging Research: Old Issues— New Approaches,* ed. by E. P. Stanford. San Diego: San Diego State University, 1979. See also: Theory, Research, and Training.

1089. _____. "Triple Jeopardy: Underserved Hispanic Elders." *Generations*, 6, no. 3 (Spring 1982): 25, 58.

1090. _____. "Why Have Hispanic Senior Programs Been Getting the Butt End?" *Somos*, 1, no. 5 (1978): 15-17.

1091. Markides, K. S. and Rodriguez, L. "MASH in San Antonio." *Texas Nursing*, 52 (1978): 8-15.

1092. Mendoza, L. "Hispanic Helping Networks: Techniques of Cultural Support." In *Hispanic Support Systems: Mental Health Promotion Perspectives*, ed. by R. Valle and W. Vega. Sacramento: State of California, Department of Mental Health, 1980.

1093. _____. "Los Servidores: Caretakers Among the Hispanic Elderly." *Generations* (Spring 1981): 24-25.

1094. Newton, F. "Issues in Research and Service Delivery Among Mexican American Elderly." *Gerontologist*, 20 (1980): 208-13. See also: Theory, Research, and Training.

1095. Ruhig, T. "The Migrant Hispanic Elderly: How Can They Best Be Served?" *Somos*, 1, no. 5 (1978): 32-34, 39.

1096. Salcido, R. M. "Problems of the Mexican-American Elderly in an Urban Setting." *Social Casework* (1979): 609-15.

1097. Solis, F. "Cultural Factors in Programming of Services for Spanish-Speaking Elderly." In *The National Conference on the Spanish-Speaking Elderly*, ed. by A. Hernandez and J. Mendoza. Kansas City: National Chicano Social Planning Council, 1975.

1098. Sotomayor, M. "Alternative Models of Service Delivery for the Hispanic Elderly." *Research Bulletin of the Hispanic Research Center, Fordham University*, 3 (1980): 7-10.

1099. Steglich, W.; Cartwright, W.; and Crouch, B. *Survey of Needs and Resources Among Aged Mexican Americans*. Lubbock: Texas Tech College, 1968.

1100. Tamez, H. and Hyslin, N. G. "Amigos Del Valle." *Aging* (March-April, 1980): 14-19.

1101. U.S. Senate Special Committee on Aging. *Availability and Usefulness of Federal Programs and Services to Elderly Mexican-Americans, Parts 1-5*. Washington, D.C.: U.S. Government Printing Office, 1969-1970.

1102. Villaverde, R. "Multiservice Center." In *The National Conference on the Spanish-Speaking Elderly*, ed. by A. Hernandez and J. Mendoza. Kansas City: National Chicano Social Planning Council, 1975.

1103. Woerner, L. "The Hispanic Elderly: Meeting the Needs of a Special Population." *The Civil Rights Digest* (Spring, 1979): 3-11.

1104. Zammaripa, J. "Centro-Del Barrio, Inc. Mutural Aid and Self-Help (MASH) Project." In *Black/Chicano Elderly: Service Delivery Within A Cultural Context*, ed. by R. Wright. Arlington, Texas: Graduate School of Social Work, University of Texas at Arlington, 1980.
See also 411.

Theory, Research, and Training

1105. Camarillo, M. R. "Areas for Research on Chicano Aging." In *Minority Aging: Institute on Minority Aging Proceedings*, ed. by E. P. Stanford. San Diego: San Diego State University, 1974.

1106. Carp, F. "Communicating With Elderly Mexican-Americans." *Gerontologist*, 9 (1970): 124-26. See also: Support Services and Service Delivery.

1107. Cuellar, J. B. "On the Relevance of Ethnographic Methods: Studying Aging in an Urban Mexican-American Community." In *Gerontological Research and Community Concern: A Case Study of a Multidisciplinary Project*, ed. by V. Bengtson. Los Angeles: The Ethel Percy Andrus Gerontology Center, University of Southern California, 1974.

1108. _____. "Social Science Research in the U.S. Mexican Community: A Case Study." *Aztlan*, 12, no. 1 (Spring, 1981): 1-21.

1109. Finley, G., and Delgado, M. "Formal Education and Intellectual Functioning in the Immigrant Cuban Elderly." *Experimental Aging Research*, 5, no. 2 (1979): 149-54.

1110. Galarza, E. "Forecasting Future Cohorts of Mexicano Elders." In *Chicano Aging and Mental Health*, ed. by M. Miranda and R. Ruiz. U.S. Department of Health and Human Services, 1981.

1111. Korte, A. O. "Interpretive Research Approaches and the Mexican Elders." In *Minority Aging Research: Old Issues—New Approaches*, ed. by E. P. Stanford. San Diego: San Diego State University, 1979.

1112. Lacayo, C. G. "Research and the Hispanic Elderly." In *Comprehensive Service Delivery Systems for the Minority Aged*, ed. by E. P. Stanford. San Diego: San Diego State University, 1977.

1113. Markides, K. S.; Dickson, H. D.; and Pappas, C. "Characteristics of Dropouts in Longitudinal Research on Aging: A Study of Mexican Americans and Anglos." *Experimental Aging Research*, 8, nos. 3-4 (1982): 163-67.

1114. Markides, K. S.; Hoppe, S. K.; Martin, H. W.; and Timbers, D. M. "Sample Representations in a Three Generation Study of Mexican Americans." *Journal of Marriage and the Family*, 45, no. 4 (November 1983).

1115. Miranda, M., and Ruiz, R. "Research on the Chicano Elderly: Theoretical and Methodological Issues." In *Chicano Aging and Mental Health*, ed. by M. Miranda and R. Ruiz. U.S. Department of Health and Human Services, 1981.

1116. Santisteban, D., and Szapocznik, J. "Adaptation of the Multidimensional Functional Assessment Questionnaire for Use With Hispanic Elders." *Hispanic Journal of Behavioral Sciences*, 3, no. 3 (1981): 301-8.

1117. Welch, S.; Cromer, J.; and Steinman, M. "Interviewing in a Mexican-American Community: An Investigation of Some Potential Sources of Response Bias." *Public Opinion Quarterly*, 37 (1973): 115-26.

See also 452, 478, 479.

Women

1118. Elsasser, N., MacKenzie, K., and Tixier y Vigil, Y. *Las Mujeres: Conversations from a Hispanic Community*. New York: Feminist Press, 1980. See also: *Marriage and Family*.

1119. Melville, M. B., ed. *Twice a Minority: Mexican American Women*. St. Louis: C. V. Mosby, 1980.

1120. Mindiola, T. "The Cost of Being a Mexican Female Worker in the 1970 Houston Labor Market." *Aztlan*, 11, no. 2 (1980): 231-47. See also: Work and Retirement.

1121. Stephens, R.; Oser, G.; and Blau, Z. "To be Aged, Hispanic, and Female." In *Twice a Minority: Mexican-American Women*, ed by M. B. Melville. St. Louis: C. V. Mosby, 1980.

Work and Retirement

1122. Doherty, R. P. "Mexican-Americans: Growing Old in the Barrio." In *Employment Prospects of Aged Blacks, Chicanos, and Indians*. Washington, D.C.: National Council on the Aging, 1971.

1123. Garcia-Mohr, M. "The Relation of the Mexican-American Elderly's History, Language and Family System to Post-Retirement Programs." In *Retirement: Concepts and Realities*, ed. by E. P. Stanford. San Diego: San Diego State University, 1978. See also: Marriage and Family.

1124. Lacayo, C. G. "An Hispanic Perspective on Pre-Retirement Planning: 'To Plan for Tomorrow, One Must be Able to Cope with Today.'" In *Retirement: Concepts and Realities*, ed. by E. P. Stanford. San Diego: San Diego State University, 1978.

1125. _____. "Older Hispanic Workers: A Perspective." *Generations*, 6, no. 4 (Summer, 1982): 26, 67.

1126. Markides, K. S. "Reasons for Retirement and Adaptation to Retirement by Elderly Mexican-Americans." *Retirement: Concepts and Realities of Minority Elders*, ed. by E. P. Stanford. San Diego: San Diego State University, 1978.

1127. Mendoza, L. "The Role and Value of the Latino Natural Helper in Retirement." In *Retirement: Concepts and Realities*, ed. by E. P. Stanford. San Diego: San Diego State University, 1978.

1128. Mirande, A. "Familism and Participation in Government Work-Training Programs Among Chicano Aged." *Hispanic Journal of Behavioral Sciences*, 2, no. 4 (December 1980): 355-73.

1129. Moore, J. W. "Retirement and the Mexican-American Aged." *Proceedings of the NICHD Conference on Ethnic Differences in Retirement*. Tucson, Arizona, 1969.

1130. Newman, M. "A Profile of Hispanics in the U.S. Work Force." *Monthly Labor Review* (December 1978): 3-14.

1131. White House Conference on Aging. "Panel Discussion on Employment and Training: Special Concerns on the Spanish-Speaking." Washington, D.C.: U.S. Government Printing Office, 1971.

See also 515.

IV. NATIVE AMERICANS

Death and Dying

1132. Havighurst, R. "The Extent of Significance of Suicide Among American Indians Today." *Mental Hygiene, 55* (1971): 174-77. See also: Health, Medicine, and Folk Medicine; Mental Health and Life Satisfaction.

1133. Kennard, E. A. "Hopi Reactions to Death." *American Anthropologist, 39* (1937): 491-96.

1134. Kluckhohn, C. "Conceptions of Death Among the Southwestern Indians." *Culture and Behavior,* ed. by C. Kluckhohn. New York: Free Press, 1962.

1135. McIntosh, J., and Santos, J. "Suicide Among Native Americans: A Compilation of Findings." *Omega, II,* no. 4 (1980-81): 303-16.

1136. Trelease, M. "Dying Among Alaskan Indians: A Matter of Choice." In *Death: The Final Stage of Growth,* ed. by E. Kubler-Ross. Englewood Cliffs: Prentice Hall, 1975.

See also 11.

Demographic and Socioeconomic Characteristics

1137. Administration on Aging. *American Indian Population 55 Years of Age and Older: A Geographic Distribution, 1970.* Part 1, by B. S. Williams. Washington, D.C.: Administration on Aging, 1977. *See also* 1146.

1138. Administration on Aging. *Social, Economic, and Health Characteristics of Older American Indians, Part III.* Washington, D.C.: Administration on Aging, 1978. See also: Health, Medicine, and Folk Medicine.

1139. Benedict, R. "A Profile on Indian Aged." In *Minority Aged in America.* Ann Arbor: Institute of Gerontology, University of Michigan, 1972.

1140. Duin, V. N. "The Problems of Indian Poverty: The Shrinking Land Base and Ineffective Education." *Albany Law Review, 36,* no. 1 (1971): 143-81.

1141. Kunitz, S. "Factors Influencing Recent Navajo and Hopi Population Change." *Human Organization, 33* (1974): 7-16.

1142. Murdoch, S.; Schwartz, D.; and Hwang, S. "The Effects of Socioeconomic Characteristics and Off-Reservation Contacts on the Service Awareness and Usage Patterns of Elderly Native Americans." *Long Term Care and Health Services Administration Quarterly, 4,* no. 1 (1980): 64-75. See also: Support Services and Service Delivery; Health, Medicine, and Folk Medicine.

1143. Roberts, C., and Gallion, T. "Characteristics of Elderly Pueblo Indians in New Mexico." *Gerontologist, 18,* no. 5 (1978): 482-87.

1144. Sorkin, A. L. "The Economic and Social Status of the American Indian." *Journal of Negro Education, 45* (Fall, 1976).

1145. U.S. Department of Agriculture. *Rural Indian Americans in Poverty,* by H. W. Johnson. Washington, D.C.: U.S. Government Printing Office, 1969.

1146. U.S. Department of Health, Education, and Welfare, Administration on Aging. *The American Indian Population 55 Years of Age And Older: Geographic Distribution, 1970.* No. 2 by D. G. Fowles. Washington, D.C.: U.S. Government Printing Office, 1977.

1147. Williams, B. S. *Social, Economic and Health Characteristics of Older American Indians.* Washington, D.C.: National Clearinghouse on Aging, 1978. See also: Health, Medicine, and Folk Medicine.

Food and Nutrition

1148. Duncan, G. "The Inter-Tribal Council in California, Inc." In *Comprehensive Service Delivery Systems for the Minority Aged,* ed. by E. P. Stanford. San Diego: San Diego State University, 1977. See also: Support Services and Service Delivery.

1149. "Nutrition Program Aids California's Older Native Americans." *Aging* (Sept.-Oct. 1976): 11-12. See also: Support Services and Service Delivery.

General

1150. Bachtold, L., and Eckvall, K. "Current Value Orientations of American Indians in Northern California—The Hupa." *Journal of Cross-Cultural Psychology, 9* (1978): 367-75.

1151. Block, M. "Exiled Americans: The Plight of Indian Aged in the United States." In *Ethnicity and Aging: Theory, Research, and Policy,* ed. by D. E. Gelfand and A. J. Kutzik. New York: Springer, 1979.

1152. Drake, J. "Status of the Aged in Agrarian-Oriented Societies." In *The Aged in American Society,* ed. by J. Drake. New York: Ronald Press, 1958.

1153. Dukepoo, F. *The Elder American Indian.* San Diego: San Diego State University, 1980.

1154. Edwards, E.; Edwards, M.; and Daines, G. "American Indian/ Alaska Native Elderly, A Current of Vital Concern." *Journal of Gerontological Social Work,* 2 (1980): 213-24.

1155. Hedrick, H., and St. Leger, J. "The Pima River of Life." *Aging,* (Sept.-Oct. 1976): 263-64.

1156. Levy, J. E. "The Older American Indian." In *Older Rural Americans,* ed. by E. Youmans. Lexington: University of Kentucky Press, 1967.

1157. Locklear, H. H. "American Indian Myths." *Social Work,* 17 (1972): 72-80.

1158. MacDonald, P. "Chairman's Spotlight, Respect the Navajo Elderly." *Navajo Times* (Jan. 1981).

1159. Munsell, M. R. "Functions of the Aged Among Salt River Pima (Arizona)." In *Aging and Modernization,* ed. by D. O. Cowgill and L. D. Holmes. New York: Appleton-Century-Crofts, 1972.

1160. National Indian Council on Aging. *May the Circle be Unbroken: A New Decade.* Albuquerque: Final Report on the Third National Indian Conference on Aging, 1980.

1161. National Tribal Chairmen's Association. *Summary Report: National Indian Conference on Aging.* Phoenix: National Tribal Chairmen's Association, Inc., 1976.

1162. Simmons, L. *The Role of the Aged in Primitive Society.* New York: Archon Books, 1970.

1163. _____. "Aging in Preindustrial Societies." In *Handbook of Gerontology,* ed. by C. Tibbitts. Chicago: University of Chicago Press, 1960.

1164. U.S. Senate Special Committee on Aging. "Committee on Advisory Council on the Elderly American Indian." 92nd Congress, First Session. Washington, D.C.: U.S. Government Printing Office, 1971.

1165. _____. "The Older Native American." In *Developments in Aging: 1974 and January-April, 1975.* Report of the Special Committee on Aging, U.S. Senate. Washington, D.C.: U.S. Government Printing Office, 1975.

1166. White House Conference on Aging. *Reports of the Special Concerns Sessions, 1971: The Elderly Indian.* Washington, D.C.: U.S. Government Printing Office, #6, 1972.

1167. Williams, G. C. "Warriors No More: A Study of the American Indian Elderly." In *Aging in Culture and Society: Comparative Viewpoint and Strategies,* ed. by C. L. Fry. New York: J. F. Bergin, 1980.

Health, Medicine, and Folk Medicine

1168. American Indian Nurses Association. "The Environment of Elderly Native Americans." *The Continuum of Life: Health Concerns of the Indian Elderly.* Second National Indian Conference on Aging, Billings, Montana, 1978.

1169. Association of American Indian Physicians, Inc. "Physical and Mental Health of Elderly American Indians." *The Continuum of Life: Health Concerns of the Indian Elderly.* Second National Indian Conference on Aging, Billings, Montana, 1978. See also: Mental Health and Life Satisfaction.

1170. Beasley, R.; Retailliau, H.; and Healey, L. "Prevalence of Rheumatoid Arthritis in Alaskan Eskimos." *Arthritis and Rheumatism,* 16 (1973): 737-42.

1171. Bennet, P.; Burch, T.; and Miller, M. "Diabetes Mellitus and American (Pima) Indians." *Lancet,* 2 (1971): 125-28.

1172. Bolesta, L. M. "The Health Status of Alaska's Native Aging and Aged Population." In *The Indian Elder: A Forgotten American.* Washington, D.C.: National Tribal Chairmen's Association, 1978.

1173. Clifford, N., et al. "Coronary Heart Disease and Hypertension in the White Mountain Apache Tribe." *Circulation,* 28 (1963): 926-31.

1174. Cohen, B. "Arterial Hypertensions Among Indians of the Southwestern United States." *American Journal of Medical Sciences,* 225 (1953): 505-13.

1175. Fields, S. "Folk Healing for the Wounded Spirit." *Innovations,* 3 (1975): 2-18.

1176. Fulmer, H. S., and Roberts, R. W. "Coronary Heart Disease Among the Navajo Indians." *Annals of Internal Medicine,* 59, no. 5 (1963): 740-64.

1177. Gutmann, D. "Navajo Dependency and Illness." In *Prediction of Life Span,* ed. by E. Palmore. Lexington, Massachusetts: Heath, 1971.

1178. Hamman, R.; Bennet, P.; and Miller, M. "Incidence of Diabetes Among the Pima Indians." *Advances in Metabolic Disorders,* 9 (1978): 49-63.

1179. Handelman, D. "Transcultural Shamanic Healing: A Washo Example." *Ethnos,* 32 (1967): 149-66.

1180. Hesse, F. G. "Incidence of Disease in the Navajo Indian: A Necropsy Study of Coronary and Aortic Atherosclerosis, Cholelithiasis, and Neoplastic Disease." In *Health Problems in U.S. and North American Indian Populations*, ed. by D. Rabin, et al. New York: MSS Information Corporation, 1972.

1181. Ingelfinger, J., et al. "Coronary Heart Disease in the Pima Indians: Electrocardiographic Findings and Postmortem Evidence of Myocardial Infarction in a Population with a High Prevalence of Diabetes Mellitus." *Diabetes, 25* (1976): 361-65.

1182. Kniep-Hardy, M., and Burkhardt, M. "Nursing the Navajo." *American Journal of Nursing, 77* (1977): 95-96.

1183. Knowler, W., et al. "Diabetes Incidence and Prevalence in Pima Indians: A 19-fold Greater Incidence than in Rochester, Minnesota." *American Journal of Epidemiology, 108* (1978): 497-505.

1184. Knowler, W.; Bennet, P.; and Ballantine, E. "Increased Incidence of Retinopathy in Diabetics with Elevated Blood Pressure: A Six-year Followup Study in Pima Indians." *New England Journal of Medicine, 302* (1980): 645-50.

1185. Knowler, W.; Bennet, P.; and Bottazzo, G. "Islet Cell Antibodies and Diabetes in Pima Indians." *Diabetologia, 17* (1979): 161-64.

1186. Knowler, W.; Pettitt, D.; Savage, P.; and Bennet, P. "Diabetes Incidence in Pima Indians: Contributions of Obesity and Parental Diabetes." *American Journal of Epidemiology, 113* (1981): 144-56.

1187. Kunitz, S.; Temkin-Greener, H.; Broudy, D.; and Haffner, M. "Determinants of Hospital Utilization and Surgery on the Navajo Indian Reservation: 1972-1973." *Social Science and Medicine, 15* (1981): 71-79.

1188. Page, I.; Lewis, L.; and Gilbert, J. "Plasma Lipids and Proteins and Their Relationship to Coronary Disease Among Navajo Indians." *Circulation, 13* (1956): 675-79.

1189. Porvasnick, J. "Recent Experiences with Cancer on the Navajo-Hopi Reservation." The *Tuba City Indian Hospital Bulletin, 3* (1962).

1190. Primeaux, M. "Caring for the American Indian Patient." *American Journal of Nursing, 77*, no. 1 (1977): 91-94.

1191. Rabin, D., et al. *Health Problems of U.S. and North American Indian Populations*. New York: MSS Information Corporation, 1972.

1192. Second National Indian Conference on Aging. *The Continuum of Life: Health Concerns of the Indian Elderly.* Billings, Montana: Second National Indian Conference on Aging, 1978.

1193. Sievers, M. "Myocardial Infarction Among Southwestern American Indians." *Annals of Internal Medicine, 67* (1967): 800-7.

1194. Streeper, R., et al. "An Electrocardiographic and Autopsy Study of Coronary Heart Disease in the Navajo." *Diseases of the Chest, 38* (1960): 305-12. See also: Mortality.

1195. Strotz, C., and Shorr, G. "Hypertension in the Papago Indians." *Circulation, 48* (1973): 1299-1303.

1196. Townsend, J. G. "Indian Health—Past, Present, and Future." In *The Changing Indian,* ed. by O. LaFarge. Norman: University of Oklahoma Press, 1942.

1197. Valory, D. "The Focus of Indian Shaker Healing." *Kroeber Anthropological Society Papers, 35* (1966): 67-111.

1198. Vogel, V. J. *American Indian Medicine.* Norman: University of Oklahoma Press, 1970.

1199. West, K. "Diabetes, Obesity and Vascular Disease in Elderly Indians." *The Continuum of Life: Health Concerns of the Indian Elderly.* Billings, Montana: Second National Indian Conference on Aging, 1978.

Life History

1200. Neihardt, J. G. *Black Elk Speaks.* New York: Simon Schuster, 1959.

1201. Nino, C. *The First Hundred Years of Nino Cochise: The Untold Story of an Apache Indian Chief.* New York: Abeland and Schuman, 1971.

Marriage and Family

1202. Deal, P. "Cultural Heritage Valued by Navajo Foster Grandparents." *Generations, 2,* no. 2 (1977): 27.

1203. Eggan, F. "Cheyenne and Arapahoe Kinship System." In *Social Anthropology of North American Tribes,* ed. by F. Eggan. Chicago: University of Chicago Press, 1955.

1204. McAllister, J. G. "Kiowa-Apache Social Organization." In *Social Anthropology of North American Tribes,* ed. by F. Eggan. Chicago: University of Chicago Press, 1955.

1205. Murdock, S., and Schwartz, D. "Family Structure and the Use of Agency Services: An Examination of Patterns Among Elderly Native Americans." *Gerontologist*, 18, no. 5, pt. 1 (1978): 475-81. See also: Support Services and Service Delivery.

1206. Opler, M. E. "An Outline of Chiricahua Apache Social Organization." In *Social Anthropology of North American Tribes*, ed. by F. Eggan. Chicago: University of Chicago Press, 1955.

1207. Price, J. A. "North American Indian Families." In *Ethnic Families in America: Patterns and Variations*. 2d ed., ed. by C. H. Mindel and R. W. Habenstein. New York: Elsevier, 1981.

1208. Red Horse, J. G. "American Indian Elders: Unifiers of Indian Families." *Social Casework*, 61, no. 8 (1980): 490-93. See also: Support Services and Service Delivery.

1209. Red Horse, J. G.; Lewis, R.; Feit, M.; and Decker, J. "Family Behavior of Urban American Indians." *Social Casework*, 59 (1978): 67-72.

1210. Red Horse, J. G. "Family Structure and Value Orientation in American Indians." *Social Casework*, 61, no. 8 (1980): 462-67.

1211. Tefft, S. K. "Intergenerational Value Differentials and Family Structure Among the Wind River Shoshone." *American Anthropologist*, 1 (1968): 330-33.

Mental Health and Life Satisfaction

1212. Hutchinson, S. H. "A Minority Under the Microscope: The American Indian Reaction." *Mental Health and Society*, 2 (1975): 181-88.

1213. Levy, J. E., and Kunitz, S. F. "Indian Reservations, Anomie and Social Pathologies." *Southwestern Journal of Anthropology*, 2 (1971): 97-128.

1214. Manson, S. M., and Pambrun, A. M. "Social and Psychological Status of the American Indian Elderly: Past Research, Current Advocacy, and Future Inquiry." *White Cloud Journal*, 1, no. 3 (1979): 18-25. See also: Theory, Research, and Training.

Mortality

1215. Carr, B., and Lee, E. "Navajo Tribal Mortality: A Life Table Analysis of the Leading Causes of Death." *Social Biology* (1978): 279-87. See also: Health, Medicine, and Folk Medicine.

1216. Hill, C. A. "Measures of Longevity of American Indians." *Public Health Reports*, 85, no. 3 (1970): 233-40. See also: Health, Medicine, and Folk Medicine.

1217. Hill, C., and Spector, M. "Natality and Mortality of American Indians compared with U.S. Whites and Nonwhites." *HSMHA Health Reports*, 86 (1971): 229-46. See also: Demographic and Socioeconomic Characteristics.

1218. Maynard, J.; Hammes, L.; and Kester, F. "Mortality due to Heart Disease among Alaskan Natives." *Public Health Reports*, 82 (1967): 714-20. See also: Health, Medicine, and Folk Medicine.

Nursing Homes and Institutionalization

1219. Red Horse, J. G. "American Indian Elders: Needs and Aspirations in Institutionalization and Home Health Care." In *Minority Aging: Policy Issues for the '80's*, ed. by E. P. Stanford. San Diego: San Diego State University, 1980. See also: Support Services and Service Delivery.

1220. Shomaker, D. M. "Navajo Nursing Homes: Conflict of Philosophies." *Journal of Gerontological Nursing*, 1, no. 9 (1981): 531-36.

Prejudice, Discrimination, Racism, and Stereotyping

1221. Jeffries, W. R. "Our Aged Indians." In *Triple Jeopardy—Myth or Reality*. Washington, D.C.: National Council on Aging, 1972.

Rural

1222. U.S. Department of Agriculture. *Rural Indian Americans in Poverty*. Washington, D.C.: U.S. Government Printing Office, 1969. See also: Demographic and Socioeconomic Characteristics.

1223. Weaver, T. *Indians in Rural and Reservation Areas: Report for the California State Advisory Commission on Indian Affairs*. Sacramento: State of California Printing Office, 1966.

Social Policy and Politics

1224. Curley, L. "Indian Elders: A Failure of Aging Policy." *Generations*, 6, no. 3 (Spring 1982): 38, 52.

1225. _____. "Title VI of the Older Americans Act, 'Grants to Indian Tribes.'" In *Minority Aging Research: Old Issues—New Approaches*, ed. by E. P. Stanford. San Diego: San Diego State University, 1979.

1226. De Montigny, L. H. "The Bureaucratic Game and a Proposed Indian Ploy." *Indian Historian*, 8 (1975): 25-30.

1227. Deloria, V. "The War Between the Redskins and the Feds." In *The Indian in American History*, ed. by F. P. Pricha. New York: Holt, Rinehart, and Winston, 1971.

1228. Flemming, A. "National Indian Conference on Aging–Excerpts from Keynote Address and Answers to Questions." In *The Indian Elder, A Forgotten American*. Albuquerque: National Tribal Chairman's Association, Inc. National Indian Conference on Aging, 1978.

1229. Lyon, J. P. "The Indian Elder: A Forgotten American." *Final Report on the First National Indian Conference on Aging*. Washington, D.C.: National Tribal Chairmen's Association, 1976.

1230. Red Horse, J. "American Indian and Alaskan Native Elders: A Policy Critique." In *Understanding Minority Aging: Perspectives and Sources*, ed. by J. B. Cuellar, E. P. Stanford, and D. I. Miller-Soule. San Diego: San Diego State University, 1982.

1231. White House Conference on Aging. *The Elderly Indian: Toward A National Policy on Aging*. Final Report, vol. 2, 1971.

Social Security and Old Age Assistance

1232. Schmulowitz, J., and Bell, R. "American Indian SSI Recipients in Selected Areas." *Social Security, 40* (1977): 42-46.

Support Services and Service Delivery

1233. Castro, T. "Crisis of the Urban Indian." *Human Needs* (1972): 29-30.

1234. Cooley, R.; Ostendorf, D.; and Bickerton, D. "Notes for Practice: Outreach Services for Elderly Native Americans." *Social Work, 24* (1979): 151-53.

1235. Edwards, E. D., et al. *Directory of Agencies Serving the Native American Aged*. Salt Lake City: School of Social Work, University of Utah, 1978.

1236. Farris, C. E. "American Indian Social Worker Advocates." *Social Casework, 57* (1976): 494-503.

1237. Good Tracks, J. G. "Native Noninterference." *Social Work, 18* (1973): 30-35.

1238. Hines, C. *Elderly Alaskan Natives in Anchorage: A Needs-Assessment for Social Services Program Planning*. Anchorage: University of Alaska Press, 1979.

1239. Levitan, S., and Hetrick, B. "Big Brother's Last Stand." *Poverty and Human Resources, 5* (1970): 5-13. See also: Support Services and Service Delivery.

1240. Long, H. "The Older American Indian—Some Considerations." In *Minority Aging*, ed. by E. P. Stanford. San Diego: San Diego State University, 1974.

1241. National Indian Council on Aging. "Data and Materials to Support a Community Education and Safety Program to Reduce Accidents Among Elderly Indians." In *The Continuum of Life: Health Concerns of the Indian Elderly*. Billings, Montana: Second National Indian Conference on Aging, 1978. See also: Health, Medicine, and Folk Medicine.

1242. Poppy, M. "Needs Assessment in Minority Aging Research." In *Minority Aging Research: Old Issues—New Approaches*, ed. by E. P. Stanford. San Diego: San Diego State University, 1979.

1243. "Projects in Nevada Succeed in Helping Indians Help Themselves." *Aging* (Sept.-Oct. 1976): 18-20.

1244. Woodenlegs, J. *Protective Services for Elderly American Indians*. Billings, Montana: Second National Conference on Aging, 1978.

Theory, Research, and Training

1245. American Indian Nurses Association. "Alternatives for Planning a Continuum of Care for Elderly American Indians." *The Continuum of Life: Health Concerns of the Indian Elderly*. Billings, Montana: Second National Indian Conference on Aging, 1978. See also: Theory, Research, and Training.

1246. Bahr, H.; Chadwick, B.; and Day, R., eds. *Native Americans Today: Sociological Perspectives*. New York: Harper and Row, 1972.

1247. Eggan, F., ed. *Social Anthropology of North American Tribes*. Chicago: University of Chicago Press, 1955.

1248. Goldstine, T., and Gutmann, D. "A TAT Study of Navajo Aging." *Psychiatry*, *35*, no. 4 (1972): 373-84. See also: Theory, Research, and Training.

Women

1249. Hanson, W. "The Urban Indian Woman and Her Family." *Social Casework*, *51*, no. 8 (1980): 476-83. See also: Marriage and Family; Rural.

1250. Richek, H. G.; Chuculate, O.; and Klinert, D. "Aging and Ethnicity in Healthy Elderly Women." *Geriatrics*, *26*, no. 5 (1971): 146-52. See also: Health, Medicine, and Folk Medicine.

Work and Retirement

1251. Curley, L. "Retirement: An Indian Perspective." In *Retirement: Concepts and Realities*, ed. by E. P. Stanford. San Diego: San Diego State University, 1978.

1252. Doherty, R. P. "Growing Old in Indian Country." In *Employment Prospects of Aged Blacks, Chicanos, and Indians*. Washington, D.C.: National Council on the Aging, 1971.

1253. National Indian Council on Aging. "Employment and the Elderly." *National Indian Council on Aging Quarterly*, *1*, no. 1 (1981): 2-5.

See also 515.

V. ASIAN AND PACIFIC AMERICANS

Death and Dying

1254. Ibrahim, I.; Carter, C.; McLaughlin, D.; and Rashad, M. "Ethnicity and Suicide in Hawaii." *Social Biology,* 24 (1977): 10-16.

1255. Kalish, R. "Suicide: An Ethnic Comparison in Hawaii." *Bulletin of Suicidology* (December 1968): 37-43.

1256. Yamamoto, J. "Japanese-American Suicides in Los Angeles." In *Anthropology and Mental Health,* ed. by J. Westermeyer. The Hague: Mouton Publishers, 1976.

General

1257. Berrien, F. K.; Arkoff, A.; and Iwahara, S. "Generation Difference in Values of Americans, Japanese Americans, and Japanese." *Journal of Social Psychology,* 71 (1967): 169-75.

1258. Bessents, T. E. "An Aging Issei Anticipates Rejection." In *Clinical Studies in Cultural Conflict,* ed. by G. Steward. New York: Ronald Press, 1958.

1259. Chandler, A. R. "The Traditional Chinese Attitude Toward Old Age." *Journal of Gerontology,* 4 (1949): 239-44.

1260. Chen, P-N. "The Chinese Community in Los Angeles." *Social Casework,* 51 (1970): 591-98.

1261. Cheng, E. *The Elder Chinese.* San Diego: San Diego State University, 1978.

1262. Connor, J. W. "Summary and Conclusions." In *Tradition and Change in Three Generations of Japanese Americans.* Chicago: Nelson-Hall, 1977.

1263. Connor, J. W. "Value Continuities and Change in Three Generations of Japanese Americans." *Ethos,* 2 (1974): 232-64.

1264. Fong, S. "Assimilation of Chinese in America: Changes in Orientation and Social Perception." *American Journal of Sociology,* 63 (1970): 265-73.

1265. Hosokawa, B. *Nisei: The Quiet Americans.* New York: William Morrow, 1969.

1266. Iklers, C. *Aging and Adaptation: The Chinese in Hong Kong and Greater Boston.* Hamden, Conn.: Archon, 1983.

1267. Ishikawa, W. H. *The Elder Guamanian.* San Diego: San Diego State University, 1978.

1268. _____. *The Elder Samoan.* San Diego: San Diego State University, 1978.

1269. Ishizuka, K. *The Elder Japanese.* San Diego: San Diego State University, 1978.

1270. Ito, A. "The Japanese Elderly." In *Minority Aging,* ed. by E. P. Stanford. San Diego: San Diego State University, 1975.

1271. _____. "Keiro Nursing Home: A Study of Japanese Cultural Adaptations." In *Minority Aging,* ed. by E. P. Stanford. San Diego: San Diego State University, 1974.

1272. Kalish, R. A., and Moriwaki, S. "The World of the Elderly Asian American." *Journal of Social Issues,* 29 (1973): 187-209.

1273. Kalish, R. A., and Yuen, S. Y. "Americans of East Asian Ancestry: Aging and the Aged." *Gerontologist,* 11, no. 1 (1971): 36-47.

1274. Kamikawa, L. "Expanding Perception of Aging: The Pacific/Asian Elderly." *Generations,* 6, no. 3 (1982): 26-27.

1275. Kitagawa, D. *Issei and Nisei: The Internment Years.* New York: Seabury Press, 1967.

1276. Kitano, H. H. L. *Japanese Americans: The Evolution of a Subculture.* 2d ed. Englewood Cliffs: Prentice-Hall, 1976.

1277. Kotchek, L. " 'Of Course We Respect Our Old People, But . . .' Aging Among Samoan Migrants." *California Sociologist,* 3, no. 2 (1980): 197-212.

1278. Lee, P., and Takamura, J. "The Japanese-Americans in Hawaii." *Cross Culture Caring* (1980): 95-120.

1279. Lyman, S. *The Asian in North America.* Santa Barbara: Clio Press, 1977.

1280. _____. "Japanese American Generation Gap." *Society,* 10 (1973): 55-63.

1281. Masuda, M.; Matsumoto, G.; and Meredith, G. M. "Ethnic Identity in Three Generations of Japanese Americans." *Journal of Social Psychology,* 81 (1970): 199-207.

1282. Matsumoto, G.; Meredith, G.; and Masuda, M. "Ethnic Identification: Honolulu and Seattle Japanese Americans." *Journal of Cross-Cultural Psychology,* 1, no. 1 (1970): 63-76.

1283. Montero, D. "The Elderly Japanese American: Aging Among the First Generation Immigrants." *Genetic Psychology Monographs, 1* (1980): 99-118.

1284. _____. *Japanese Americans: Changing Patterns of Ethnic Affiliation Over Three Generations.* Boulder, Colorado: Westview, 1980.

1285. Nee, V., and Nee, B. *Long Time Califon': A Documentary Study of an American Chinatown.* New York: Pantheon, 1973.

1286. Nusberg, C., and Osako, M. *The Situation of the Asian/Pacific Elderly.* Washington, D.C.: International Federation on Aging, 1981.

1287. Peralta, V. "The Asian American Elderly in Greater Philadelphia: A Neglected Minority." *Bridge: An Asian American Perspective,* 6, no. 2 (1978): 50-53.

1288. Peterson, R. *The Elder Pilipino.* San Diego: San Diego State University, 1978.

1289. Sacks, J. *Chinese-Americans.* Gerontology Planning Project, School of Education. Amherst: University of Massachusetts, 1979.

1290. Weiss, M. S., ed. *Chinese Communities in America.* Boston: Schenkman, 1972.

1291. White House Conference on Aging. *The Asian American Elderly.* Washington, D.C.: U.S. Government Printing Office, 1972.

1292. Wu, F. "Mandarin-Speaking Chinese in the Los Angeles Area." *Gerontologist, 15* (1975): 271-75.
See also 97.

Health, Medicine, and Folk Medicine

1293. Bennett, C. G.; Tokuyama, G. H.; and Bruyere, R. P. "Health of Japanese Americans in Hawaii." *Public Health Reports,* United States Public Health Service (1963): 753-62.

1294. Campbell, T., and Chang, B. "Health Care of the Chinese in America." *Nursing Outlook, 21* (1973): 245-49.

1295. Carp, F., and Katoaka, E. "Health Care Problems of the Elderly in San Francisco's Chinatown." *Gerontologist, 16,* part I (1976): 30-38.

1296. Cattell, S. *Health, Welfare and Social Organization in Chinatown, New York City.* New York: Dept. of Public Affairs, 1962.

1297. Constantino, M. "Health Status of the Filipino Elderly." In *Minority Aging Research: Old Issues—New Approaches,* ed. by E. P. Stanford. San Diego: San Diego State University, 1979.

1298. Hessler, R. M.; Nolan, M. F.; Ogbru, B.; and New, P. K-M. "Intra-ethnic Diversity: Health Care of the Chinese-Americans." *Human Organization*, *34*, no. 3 (1975): 253-62.

1299. Kagan, A., et al. "Epidemiologic Studies of Coronary Heart Diseases and Stroke in Japanese Men Living in Japan, Hawaii and California: Demographic, Physical, Dietary and Biochemical Characteristics." *Journal of Chronic Diseases*, *27* (1974): 345-64.

1300. Kato, H.; Tillotson, J.; Nichaman, M. A.; Rhoads, G. G.; and Hamilton, H. B. "Epidemiologic Studies of Coronary Heart Disease and Stroke in Japanese Men Living in Japan, Hawaii and California." *American Journal of Epidemiology*, *97*, no. 6 (1973): 372-85.

1301. Kawate, R.; Yamakido, M.; Nashimote, Y.; et al. "Diabetes Mellitus and Its Vascular Complications in Japanese Migrants on the Island of Hawaii." *Diabetes Care*, *2* (1979): 161-70.

1302. Lee, I. C. "Health Care Needs of the Elderly Chinese in Los Angeles, with a Socio-Cultural Orientation." *Asian Profile*, *7*, no. 2 (1979): 119-30.

1303. U.S. Department of Health, Education and Welfare. *Summary Report of the National Symposium on High Blood Pressure Control in U.S. Asian and Pacific Populations.* Washington, D.C., 1979.
See also 255.

Marriage and Family

1304. Connor, J. W. "Acculturation and Family Continuities in Three Generations of Japanese Americans." *Journal of Marriage and the Family*, *36*, no. 1 (1974): 159-65.

1305. Huang, L. J. "The Chinese American Family." In *Ethnic Families in America.* 2d ed., ed. by C. H. Mindel and R. W. Habenstein. New York: Elsevier, 1981.

1306. Johnson, O. L. "Interdependence, Reciprocity and Indebtedness: An Analysis of Japanese American Kinship Relations." *Journal of Marriage and the Family*, *39*, no. 2 (1977): 351-63.

1307. Kiefer, C. W. *Changing Cultures, Changing Lives: An Ethnographic Study of Three Generations of Japanese Americans.* San Francisco: Jossey-Bass Publishers, 1974.

1308. Kikumura, A. and Kitano, H. H. L. "The Japanese American Family." In *Ethnic Families in America.* 2d ed., ed. by C. H. Mindel and R. W. Habenstein. New York: Elsevier, 1981.

1309. Kobata, F. "The Influence of Culture on Family Relations: The Asian American Experience." In *Aging Parents*, ed. by P. Ragan. Los Angeles: University of Southern California, 1979.

1310. Osako, M. "Aging and Family Among Japanese-Americans: The Role of Ethnic Tradition in the Adjustment to Old-Age." *Gerontologist*, *19*, no. 5 (1979): 448-55.

1311. _____. "Intergenerational Relations as an Aspect of Assimilation: The Case of the Japanese-Americans." *Sociological Inquiry*, *46* (1976): 67-72.

Mental Health and Life Satisfaction

1312. Berk, B. "Mental Illness among the Chinese: Myth or Reality?" *Journal of Social Issues*, *29* (1973): 149-66.

1313. Jew, C. C., and Brody, S. A. "Mental Illness Among the Chinese: Hospitalization Rates Over the Past Century." *Comprehensive Psychiatry*, *8* (1967): 129-34.

1314. Lum, D.; Yim-San, L.; et al. "The Psychosocial Needs of the Chinese Elderly." *Social Casework* (1980): 100-05.

1315. Ozawa, N. "Mental Health Aspects of Pacific Asians." In *Minority Aging Research: Old Issues – New Approaches*, ed. by E. P. Stanford. San Diego: San Diego State University, 1979.

1316. Sue, D., and Sue, S. "Counseling Chinese-Americans." *Personnel and Guidance Journal*, *50* (1972): 637-44.

1317. Sue, S., and Sue, D. "Chinese-American Personality and Mental Health." *Amerasia Journal*, 1 (1971): 36-49.

1318. Wong, E. F. "Learned Helplessness: The Need for Self-Determination Among the Chinese American Elderly." *Journal of Ethnic Studies*, 8, no. 2 (1980): 45-62.

1319. Yuen, S. "Aging and Mental Health in San Francisco's Chinatown." In *Ethnicity, Mental Health, and Aging*. Los Angeles: The Ethel Percy Andrus Gerontology Center, University of Southern California, 1970.

Mortality

1320. Bell, B. Z. "Mortality and Morbidity of the Native Hawaiians." Report no. 5, Scholar in Residence Program. Pacific/Asian American Mental Health Research Center, Chicago, Illinois, 1978. See also: Health, Medicine, and Folk Medicine.

1321. Gordon, T. "Further Mortality Experience among Japanese Americans." *Public Health Reports, 82* (1967): 973-84.

Prejudice, Discrimination, Racism, and Stereotyping

1322. Fujii, S. "Older Asian Americans: Victims of Multiple Jeopardy." *Civil Rights Digest* (Fall 1976): 22-29.

1323. Petersen, W. *Japanese Americans: Oppression and Success.* New York: Random House, 1971.

1324. U.S. Commission of Civil Rights. *Asian Americans and Pacific Peoples: A Case of Mistaken Identity.* Washington, D.C.: 1975.

1325. _____. *The Forgotten Minority: Asian Americans in New York City.* Washington, D.C.: 1977.

Social Policy and Politics

1326. Ishikawa, W. H. "Pacific Asian Elderly." *Policy Issues Concerning the Minority Elderly: Final Report, Six Papers.* San Francisco: Human Resources Corporation, 1978.

1327. Kiefer, C. "Lessons from the Issei." In *Late Life: Community and Environmental Policy,* ed. by J. Gubrium. Springfield: C. C. Thomas, 1974.

1328. Moriwaki, S. Y. "Update of Current Status of and Future Direction for Ethnic Minority Elderly Groups: Pacific/Asians." In *Understanding Minority Aging: Perspectives and Sources,* ed. by J. B. Cuellar, E. P. Stanford, and D. I. Miller-Soule. San Diego: San Diego State University, 1982.

1329. White House Conference on Aging. Reports of the Special Concerns Sessions. *Recommended for Action: The Asian American Elderly.* Washington, D.C.: U.S. Government Printing Office, 1972.

Support Services and Service Delivery

1330. Arkoff, A. "Need Patterns in Two Generations of Japanese Americans in Hawaii." *Journal of Social Psychology, 50* (1959): 75-79.

1331. Chinn, G., and Newcomb, L. *On the Feasibility of Training Asians to Work with Asian Elderly: A Preliminary Assessment of Needs and Resources Available to Asian Elderly in Seattle, Washington.* Training Project for the Asian Elderly, Seattle, Washington, 1973.

1332. Cohen, A. "Developing Comprehensive Services for the Chinese American Community." *Bridge: An Asian American Perspective, 6* (1978): 50-51.

1333. Fujii, S. "Elderly Asian Americans and Use of Public Services." *Social Casework*, 57, no. 3 (1976): 202-7.

1334. Ishikawa, W., and Archer, N. H. *Service Delivery in Pan Asian Communities: Conference Proceedings*. San Diego: Pacific Asian Coalition Mental Health Training Center, San Diego State University, 1975.

1335. Kuramoto, F. "What Do Asians Want? An Examination of Issues in Social Work Education." *Journal of Education for Social Work*, 7, no. 3 (1971): 7-17.

1336. Leung, P.; Nagasawa, R.; and Quan, A. "Asian American Awareness and Knowledge of the Problems of Asian Elderly in Arizona." Chicago: Report #15, Scholar-In-Residence Program, Pacific/Asian American Mental Health Research Center, 1979.

1337. Lyman, S. "Contrasts in the Community Organization of Chinese-Japanese in North America." *Canadian Review of Sociology and Anthropology*, 5 (1968): 51-67.

1338. Mori, S. O. "Kimochi: Good Feelings for Japanese-American Elders." *Generations*, 6, no. 3 (Spring 1982): 46, 52.

1339. Pacific/Asian Elderly Research Project. *National Directory of Services to the Pacific/Asian Elderly*. Los Angeles: Pacific/Asian Elderly Research Project, 1977.

1340. Salcido, R. M.; Nakamo, C.; and Jue, S. "The Use of Formal and Informal Health and Welfare Services of the Asian-American Elderly: An Exploratory Study." *California Sociologist*, 3, no. 2 (1980): 213-29.

1341. Yamaki, E. "Koreisha Chushoku Kai (Nutrition Program for the Elderly)." In *Comprehensive Service Delivery Systems for the Minority Aged*, ed. by E. P. Stanford. San Diego: San Diego State University, 1977.

1342. Yip, B. "Accessibility to Services for Pan-Asian Elderly: Fact or Fiction?" In *Minority Aging: Policy Issues for the '80's*, ed. by E. P. Stanford. San Diego: San Diego State University, 1980.

Theory, Research, and Training

1343. Chen, P.-N. "Study of Chinese-American Elderly Residing in Hotel Rooms." *Social Casework*, 60, no. 2 (1979): 89-95.

1344. Chen, S. C., and Chen, J. L. "Effects of Culture on the Success of Aging: A Preliminary Study Comparing the Productivity of Two Aging Groups of Chinese and American Men." *Boston Medical Quarterly*, 15 (1964): 4-22.

1345. Ishizuka, K. L. "Oral History in Social Context: Little Tokyo, Los Angeles." In *Minority Aging Research: Old Issues – New Approaches*, ed. by E. P. Stanford. San Diego: San Diego State University, 1979.

1346. Kiefer, C. W. "History and Culture as Problems of Predicting Human Adaptation: The Issei (First Generation Japanese) Case." *Gerontologist, 14*, no. 5, pt. 2 (1974): 66.

1347. Levine, G. N., and Montero, D. M. "Socioeconomic Mobility Among Three Generations of Japanese Americans." *Journal of Social Issues, 29*, no. 2 (1973): 33-48.

1348. Mizokawa, D. T. "Some Issues in Educational Gerontology of Japanese-American Elders." *Educational Gerontology, 2*, no. 2 (1977): 123-29.

1349. Montero, D. "Disengagement and Aging Among the Issei." In *Ethnicity and Aging: Theory, Research, and Policy*, ed. by D. Gelfand and A. Kutzik. New York: Springer, 1979.

1350. Pacific/Asian Elderly Research Project. *A Listing of Researchers with Experience and/or Interest in the Pacific/Asian Elderly, and Directory of Samoan Organizations, Resource Persons, and Churches of Los Angeles.* Los Angeles: Pacific/Asian Elderly Research Project, 1977.

1351. Schwitters, S. Y. "Elderly Pacific/Asians: Emerging Research Issues." In *Understanding Minority Aging: Perspectives and Sources*, ed. by J. B. Cuellar, E. P. Stanford, and D. I. Miller-Soule. San Diego: San Diego State University, 1982.

Women

1352. Gee, E. "Issei Women." In *Counterpoint: Perspectives on Asian America*, ed. by E. Gee. Los Angeles: University of California Asian American Studies Center, 1976.

1353. Sone, M. *Nisei Daughter.* Boston: Little, Brown, 1953.

1354. Timpane, M., ed. *Conference on the Educational and Occupational Needs of Asian-Pacific-American Women.* Washington, D.C.: U.S. Government Printing Office, 1980. See also: Work and Retirement.

1355. Yanagida, E., and Marsella, A. J. "The Relationship Between Depression and Self-Concept Discrepancy Among Different Generations of Japanese-American Women." *Journal of Clinical Psychology, 34*, no. 3 (July 1978): 654-59.

Work and Retirement

1356. Alegria, P. R. "Filipino Elderly." In *Retirement: Concepts and Realities*, ed. by E. P. Stanford. San Diego: San Diego State University, 1978.

1357. Alegria, P. R. "The Lifestyle of Filipino Elderly and Its Implications for Retirement." In *Retirement: Concepts and Realities*, ed. by E. P. Stanford. San Diego: San Diego State University, 1978.

1358. Fujii, S. "Elderly Pacific Island and Asian-American Women: A Framework for Understanding." In *Conference on the Educational and Occupational Needs of Asian-Pacific-American Women*, ed. by M. Timpane. Washington, D.C.: Publication no. 1980 0-629-701/2992, U.S. Government Printing Office, 1980.

1359. _____. "Retirement as it Relates to the Pacific-Asian Elderly." In *Retirement: Concepts and Realities*, ed. by E. P. Stanford. San Diego: San Diego State University, 1978.

1360. Ishizuka, K. L. "Caretaking: Implications for Nisei Retirement." In *Retirement: Concepts and Realities*, ed. by E. P. Stanford. San Diego: San Diego State University, 1978.

1361. Kwon, P. H. "Korean Elderly People's Lifestyle Old and New in the United States." In *Retirement: Concepts and Realities*, ed. by E. P. Stanford. San Diego: San Diego State University, 1978.

1362. Yip, B. C. "Chinese Elderly Lifestyles." In *Retirement: Concepts and Realities*, ed. by E. P. Stanford. San Diego: San Diego State University, 1978.

VI. EUROPEAN ORIGIN ETHNIC GROUPS

Comparative Studies of White Ethnics

1363. Cohler, B. "Stress or Support: Relations Between Older Women from Three European Ethnic Groups and Their Relatives." In *Minority Aging: Sociological and Social Psychological Issues*, ed. by R. C. Manuel. Westport, Conn.: Greenwood Press, 1982.

1364. Cohler, B., and Lieberman, M. "Personality Change Across the Second Half of Life: Findings From a Study of Irish, Italian, and Polish-American Men and Women." In *Ethnicity and Aging: Theory, Research and Policy*, ed. by D. Gelfand and A. Kutzik. New York: Springer, 1979.

1365. _____. "Social Relations and Mental Health: Middle-Aged and Older Men and Women From Three European Ethnic Groups." *Research on Aging*, 2, no. 4 (1980): 445-69.

1366. Fandetti, D., and Gelfand, D. "Care of the Aged: Attitudes of White Ethnic Families." *Gerontologist*, 16 (1976): 544-49.

1367. Gelfand, D., and Olsen, J. "Aging in the Jewish Family and the Mormon Family." In *Ethnicity and Aging: Theory, Research, and Policy*, ed. by D. Gelfand and A. Kutzik. New York: Springer, 1979.

1368. Gelfand, D., and Fandetti, D. "Suburban and Urban White Ethnics: Attitudes Toward Care of the Aged." *Gerontologist*, 20 (1980): 588-94.

1369. Guttmann, D. "Use of Informal and Formal Supports by White Ethnic Aged." In *Ethnicity and Aging: Theory, Research, and Policy*, ed. by D. Gelfand and A. Kutzik. New York: Springer, 1979.

1370. Krause, C. A. *Grandmothers, Mothers, and Daughters, An Oral History Study of Ethnicity, Mental Health, and Continuity of Three Generations of Jewish, Italian, and Slavic-American Women*. New York: The Institute on Pluralism and Group Identity of the American Jewish Committee, 1978.

1371. Kahana, E., and Felton, B. "Social Context and Personal Need: A Study of Polish and Jewish Aged." *Journal of Social Issues*, 33, no. 4 (1977): 56-74.

1372. Ryan, J., ed. *White Ethnics*. Englewood Cliffs: Prentice-Hall, 1973.

Italian Americans

1373. Bruhn, J.; Chandler, B.; Miller, M.; Wolf, S.; and Lynn, T. "Social Aspects of Coronary Heart Disease in Two Adjacent Ethnically Different Communities." *American Journal of Public Health*, 56 (1966): 1493-1506.

1374. Bruhn, J.; Philips, B.; and Wolf, S. "Social Readjustment and Illness Patterns: Comparisons Between First, Second, and Third Generation Italian-Americans Living in the Same Community." *Journal of Psychosomatic Research,* 16 (1972): 387-94

1375. Galante, F. "The Italian Family: How It Deals with Acute Grief and the Funeral." In *Acute Grief and the Funeral,* ed. by V. Pine, A. Kutschen, D. Peretz, R. Slater, R. Bellis, R. Valk, and D. Cherico. Springfield, Ill.: Charles C. Thomas, 1976.

1376. Gambino, R. "La Famiglia: Four Generations of Italian-Americans." In *White Ethnics,* ed. by J. Ryan. Englewood Cliffs: Prentice-Hall, 1973.

1377. Johnson, E. S. "Role Expectations and Role Realities of Older Italian Mothers and Their Daughters." *International Journal of Aging and Human Development,* 14, no. 4 (1981-82): 271-76.

1378. Quadagno, J. "The Italian American Family." In *Ethnic Families in America.* 2d ed., ed. by C. H. Mindel and R. W. Habenstein. New York: Elsevier, 1981.

Jewish Americans

1379. "The Aging Survivor of the Holocaust." *Journal of Geriatric Psychiatry,* 14, no. 2 (1981): 131-244.

1380. Bart, P. "Mother Portnoy's Complaints." *Trans-Action,* 8, nos. 1-2 (1970): 69-74.

1381. Berezin, M. A. "Introduction to 'The Aging Survivor of the Holocaust.'" *Journal of Geriatric Psychiatry,* 14, no. 2 (1981): 131-33.

1382. Cath, S. H. "Discussion in 'The Aging Survivor of the Holocaust.'" *Journal of Geriatric Psychiatry,* 14, no. 2 (1981): 155-63.

1383. Danieli, Y. "Discussion: On the Achievement of Integration in Aging Survivors of the Nazi Holocaust." *Journal of Geriatric Psychiatry,* 14, no. 2 (1981): 191-210.

1384. Eckardt, A. R. "Death in the Judaic and Christian Traditions." *Death in the American Experience,* ed. by A. Mack. New York: Schocken, 1973.

1385. "Ethnic Minorities: Israel; United States." *Ageing International,* 7, no. 3 (1980): 4-5.

1386. Farber, B.; Mindel, C.; and Lazerwitz, B. "The Jewish American Family." In *Ethnic Families in America,* 2d ed., ed. by C. H. Mindel and R. W. Habenstein. New York: Elsevier, 1981.

1387. Goldstein, S., and Goldscheider, C. *Jewish Americans: Three Generations in a Jewish Community.* Englewood Cliffs: Prentice-Hall, 1968.

1388. Gordon, A. "The Jewish View of Death. Guidelines for Mourning." *Death: The Final Stage of Growth,* ed. by E. Kubler-Ross. Englewood Cliffs: Prentice-Hall, 1975.

1389. Guttman, D. "Leisure-Time Activity Interests of Jewish Elderly." *Gerontologist, 13* (1973): 219-23.

1390. Herzog, J. M. "Father Hurt and Father Hunger: The Effect of a Survivor Father's Waning Years on his Son." *Journal of Geriatric Psychiatry, 14,* no. 2 (1981): 211-23.

1391. Kahana, R. J. "Discussion: Reconciliation Between the Generations: A Last Chance." *Journal of Geriatric Psychiatry, 14,* no. 2 (1981): 225-39.

1392. Kramer, S., and Masur, J. *Jewish Grandmothers.* Boston: Beacon Press, 1976.

1393. Krystal, H. "Integration and Self-Healing in Posttraumatic States." *Journal of Geriatric Psychiatry, 14,* no. 2 (1981): 165-89.

1394. Lawton, M.; Kleban, M.; and Singer, M. "The Aged Jewish Person and the Slum Environment." *Journal of Gerontology, 26* (1971): 231-39.

1395. Merowitz, M. "Words Before We Go: The Experience of the Holocaust and Its Effect on Communications in the Aging Survivor." *Journal of Geriatric Psychiatry, 14,* no. 2 (1981): 241-44.

1396. Meyerhoff, B. *Number Our Days.* New York: Dutton, 1978.

1397. Ornstein, A. "The Effects of the Holocaust on Life-Cycle Experiences: The Creation and Recreation of Families." *Journal of Geriatric Psychiatry, 14,* no. 2 (1981): 135-54.

1398. Shore, H. "The Current Social Revolution and Its Impact on Jewish Nursing Homes." *Gerontologist, 12* (1972): 178-80.

1399. Steinitz, L. Y. "Psycho-Social Effects of the Holocaust on Aging Survivors and their Families." *Journal of Gerontological Social Work, 4,* nos. 3-4 (1982): 145-52.
See also 11.

Polish Americans

1400. Lopata, H. Z. "The Polish American Family." In *Ethnic Families in America.* 2d ed., ed. by C. H. Mindel and R. W. Habenstein. New York: Elsevier, 1981.

1401. Wroebel, P. "Becoming a Polish American: A Personal Point of View." In *White Ethnics*, ed. by J. Ryan. Englewood Cliffs: Prentice-Hall, 1973.

Religious Minorities

1402. Biddle, E. H. "The American Catholic Irish Family." In *Ethnic Families in America*. 2d ed., ed. by C. H. Mindel and R. W. Habenstein. New York: Elsevier, 1981.

1403. Campbell, L., and Campbell, E. "Emergence of the Mormons as a Minority Group." In *Ethnic Families in America*. 2d ed., ed. by C. H. Mindel and R. W. Habenstein. New York: Elsevier, 1981.

1404. Hamman, R.; Barancik, J.; and Lilienfeld, A. "Patterns of Mortality in the Old Order Amish." *American Journal of Epidemiology, 114* (1981): 845-61.

1405. Huntington, G. E. "The Amish Family." In *Ethnic Families in America*. 2d ed., ed. by C. H. Mindel and R. W. Habenstein. New York: Elsevier, 1981.

Slavic Americans

1406. Krause, C. "Ethnic Culture, Religion, and the Mental Health of Slavic-American Women." *Journal of Religion and Health, 18* (1979): 298-307.

1407. Mostwin, D. "Emotional Needs of Elderly Americans of Central and Eastern European Background." In *Ethnicity and Aging: Theory, Research, and Policy*, ed. by. D. E. Gelfand and A. J. Kutzik. New York: Springer, 1979.

VII. OTHER BIBLIOGRAPHIES

Asian and Pacific Americans

1408. Pacific/Asian Elderly Research Project. "Existing Research: Part I: Bibliographies, Part II: Abstracts." Los Angeles: Pacific/Asian Elderly Research Project, 1977.

1409. White, A. G. *An Urban Minority: Japanese Americans.* Council of Planning Librarians Exchange Bibliography, No. 478. Monticello, Ill., 1973.

Blacks

1410. Davis, L. G. *The Black Aged in the United States: An Annotated Bibliography.* Westport, Conn.: Greenwood Press, 1980.

1411. Jackson, J. J. "Aged Blacks: A Selected Bibliography." In *Proceedings of the Research Conference on the Minority Group Aged in the South,* ed. by J. J. Jackson. Durham: Duke University, 1972.

1412. King, W. M. *Health, Health Care and the Black Community: An Exploratory Bibliography.* Monticello, Ill.: Council of Planning Librarians Exchange Bibliography No. 55, 1974.

1413. Lindsay, I. B. "Bibliography on the Black Aged." In U. S. Senate Committee on Aging, *The Multiple Hazards of Age and Race: The Situation of Aged Blacks in the United States.* Washington, D.C.: U.S. Government Printing Office, 1971.

Hispanics

1414. Delgado, M., and Finley, G. "The Spanish Speaking Elderly: A Bibliography." *Gerontologist,* 18, no. 4 (1978): 387-94.

1415. Department of Housing and Urban Development, Washington, D. C. Library. *Hispanic Americans in the United States: A Selective Bibliography.* Washington, D.C.: HUD, 1981.

1416. Human Resources Corporation. "The Spanish-Speaking Elderly: A Bibliography." San Francisco: The Human Resources Corporation, 1973.

1417. Torres-Gil, F. "Bibliography on the Spanish Speaking Elderly." In *The National Conference on the Spanish-Speaking Elderly,* ed. by A. Hernandez and J. Mendoza. Kansas City: National Chicano Social Planning Council, 1975.

Multiethnic

1418. Balkemas, J. B. "The Aged in Minority Groups: A Bibliography." Washington, D.C: The National Council on the Aging, 1973.

1419. Cuellar, J. B.; Stanford, E. P.; and Miller-Soule, D. I. *Understanding Minority Aging: Perspectives and Sources.* San Diego: San Diego State University, 1982.

1420. Jackson, J. J. "Partial Bibliography of Gerontological and Related Literature about Minorities—Part I. " *Black Aging, 1* (1976): 41-55.

1421. Jackson, J. J. Partial Bibliography of Gerontological and Related Literature about Minorities—Part II." *Black Aging, 2* (1976-1977): 50-65.

1422. Project Share. *Human Services for Ethnic Minorities, Revised.* Rockville, Md.: Project Share, 1981.

1423. Ragan, P. and Simonin, M. "Aging Among Blacks and Mexican Americans in the United States: A Selected Bibliography." The Ethel Percy Andrus Gerontology Center, University of Southern California, 1977.

1424. Stanford, E. P., ed. "Bibliography." In *Minority Aging: Third Institute on Minority Aging Proceedings.* San Diego: San Diego State University, 1977.

1425. Suzuki, P. T. *Minority Group Aged in America: A Comprehensive Bibliography of Recent Publications on Blacks, Mexican-Americans, Native Americans, Chinese and Japanese.* Omaha: Council of Planning Librarians, 1975.

Native Americans

1426. Barrow, M.; Niswander, J.; and Fortuine, R. *Health and Disease of American Indians North of Mexico: A Bibliography, 1800-1969.* Gainesville: University of Florida, 1972.

1427. Dobyns, H. F. *Native American Historical Demography: A Critical Bibliography.* Bloomington: Indiana University, 1976.

1428. Hodge, W. H. *A Bibliography of Contemporary North American Indians.* New York: Interland, 1976.

1429. Kerri, J. N. *American Indians (U.S. and Canada): A Bibliography of Contemporary Studies and Urban Research.* Monticello, Ill.: Council of Planning Librarians Exchange Bibliography, Nos. 376 and 377, 1971.

1430. _____. *American Indians (U.S. and Canada): A Bibliography of Contemporary Studies and Urban Research: Supplement to Council of Planning Librarians Exchange Bibliographies Nos. 376-377.* Monticello, Ill.: Council of Planning Librarians Exchange Bibliographies, No. 594, 1973.

1431. Medicine, B. "The Role of Women in Native American Studies: A Bibliography." *Indian Historian,* 8 (1975): 50-54.

1432. Murdock, G., and O'Leary, T. *Ethnographic Bibliography of North America,* 5 vols. New Haven: Human Relations Area Files, 1975.

Bibliographical Resources

To extend the shelf life and thus enhance the value of this checklist, we provide below some of the resources that can enable the user to keep the listings current. Included are the retrieval sources, both printed sources and online databases. These are followed by a list of journals in the field of aging in which forthcoming articles on ethnicity and aging will likely be found. Last is a brief compilation of journals not specifically on aging but in which future information could appear.

Retrieval sources

Printed Source	Online Database
America: History and Life	America: History and Life
ARECO's Quarterly Index to Periodical Literature on Aging (ARECO, Detroit)	
Current Literature on Aging (Washington, D. C., National Council on the Aging)	
Public Affairs Information Service Bulletin	P.A.I.S. International
Psychological Abstracts	PsycInfo
Social Sciences Index	
Social Sciences Citation Index	SOCIAL SCISEARCH
Sociological Abstracts	Sociological Abstracts

Journals in the Field of Aging

Age
Age and Aging
Aging
Aging and Human Development
 (currently called International
 Journal of Aging)
Aging and Leisure Living
Aging and Work
American Journal of Occupational
 Therapy
Annual Review of Gerontology
 and Geriatrics
Black Aging
Clinical Gerontologist
Contemporary Social Gerontology

Educational Gerontology
Experimental Aging Research
Generations
Geriatrics
Gerontological Psychology
The Gerontologist
Gerontology: International
 Journal of Experimental
 and Clinical Gerontology
Gerontology and Geriatrics
 Education
GeronTopics
Industrial Gerontology
Interdisciplinary Topics in
 Gerontology

Journals in the Field of Aging

International Journal of Aging
  and Human Development
International Journal of
  Behavioral Geriatrics
Journal of Activities,
  Adaptation, and Aging
Journal of Aging and Development
Journal of the American
  Geriatrics Society
Journal of Applied Gerontology
Journal of Geriatric Psychiatry
Journal of Gerontological
  Nursing

Journal of Gerontological
  Social Work
Journal of Gerontology
Journal of Long Term Care
  Adminstration
Journal of Minority Aging
National Council on the
  Aging Journal
Nursing Homes
Omega
Perspectives on Aging
Research on Aging
Social Security Bulletin

Other Journals

Amerasia Journal
Aztlan
Contemporary Sociology
Hispanic Journal of
  Behavioral Sciences
Journal of Black Studies

Journal of Marriage and
  Family
Phylon
Social Casework
Social Work

AUTHOR INDEX